THE OFFICIAL BETTER BRIDGE SERIES

IMPROVING YOUR JUDGMENT 2

Doubles

Audrey Grant

BARON **B**ARCLAY
BRIDGE SUPPLY

Improving Your Judgment 2: Doubles
Copyright © 2006 Audrey Grant's Better Bridge Inc.

To contact the author, see page 151.

Baron Barclay
3600 Chamberlain Lane, Suite 206
Louisville, KY 40241
U.S. and Canada: 1-800-274-2221
Worldwide: 502-426-0410
FAX: 502-426-2044
www.baronbarclay.com

ISBN 0-939460-43-2

Illustrations by Kelvin Smith
Design and composition by John Reinhardt Book Design

Printed in the United States of America

Contents

Contents

Introduction

The double is the game's most versatile call. It is especially important in today's game where competitive bidding has become so prevalent.

The best theorists in the world have shared their secrets with me. My goal is to present the most modern and complete information in a simple, straightforward style.

The *Improving Your Judgment Series* introduces each concept with examples and quizzes. At the end of each chapter are four deals incorporating the concepts discussed in the chapter along with tips on bidding, play, and defense. There are sixteen additional practice deals that cover concepts from throughout the book.

Each deal includes a suggested auction and opening lead. Since the declarer varies from deal to deal, the opening lead is underlined and the dummy is shaded to help orient yourself when following the discussion of the play and defense. The key play point is highlighted. You might find it useful to deal out the hands and place them face up on the table. There are Coded Cards available to make this easy. You can then follow the play trick by trick by turning the played cards face down. The tips on play and defense expand the usefulness of the book beyond the focus on doubles and make it a good general brush up.

If you're reading this book, you're likely an active, involved person looking for ways to efficiently improve your game. I'm confident that this book is well worth your time.

All the best,

Audrey Grant
www.AudreyGrant.com

The Bridge Basics Series

The Improving Your Judgment Series

... more to come

Acknowledgments

To my husband, *David Lindop*, a world-class player who works hand-in-hand with me to produce the bridge books.

To *Jason Grant-Lindop* and *Joanna Grant* for their support and involvement in the many aspects of Better Bridge

To the Better Bridge Advisory Committee:
- *Bob Hamman* — World Champion, top-ranked male player
- *Petra Hamman* — World Champion, bridge teacher
- *Shawn Quinn* — World Champion, top-ranked female player
- *Fred Gitelman* — Founder of Bridge Base Inc., gold medalist
- *Henry Francis* — Editor, Official Encyclopedia of Bridge
- *Jerry Helms* — Professional bridge teacher and player

To the bridge teachers. Your dedication, skill, and professionalism have made me proud to be counted among you.

To the students of the game—thank you for sharing your ideas and your enthusiasm.

The takeout double is far and away the most powerful and flexible weapon in your entire armory of defensive bids.

— Eddie Kantar, BRIDGE FOR DUMMIES

1

The Takeout Double

In every auction when it is your turn to call you have a choice between bidding a suit or notrump and passing. In a *competitive auction*, a third option becomes available, the double. It's an economical call that doesn't take up any bidding room and can be used in many auctions when other calls are unavailable or impractical.

It is most commonly used as a *takeout double* when your right-hand opponent opens the bidding. But the double can be used in many other situations. It's the game's most versatile call.

Bridge in the last century tended to focus on the *penalty double*. If partner doubled an opponent's call, you were expected to pass and defend unless you had a specific agreement to the contrary. The modern game is more competitive. Both sides are frequently in the auction. The use of the double as a competitive tool has increased in popularity. You are now generally expected to take out partner's double by bidding something unless you have another understanding.

The versatility of the double can present a challenge for the partnership. Some doubles are meant to be left in for penalties; some are meant to be taken out; some fall somewhere in between. The purpose of this book is to develop an understanding of the meaning of the double in diverse situations so that both members of the partnership can use the call with confidence.

Let's take a closer look.

The Classic Takeout Double

Our starting point will be the classic position. The player on your right opens the bidding in a suit and you double. Suppose you are South:

WEST	NORTH	EAST	SOUTH
		1♠	DOUBLE

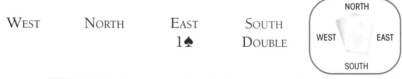

Your double of East's 1♠ opening bid is *conventionally* accepted as a takeout double, asking your partner to bid one of the *unbid suits*: hearts, diamonds, or clubs.

The basic requirements for a takeout double are:

- Values for an opening bid or more.
- Support for the unbid suits.

Let's look at the requirements for a takeout double in more detail.

Hand Valuation for a Takeout Double

There is general agreement that the value of a hand is a combination of the high cards and distribution. When you make a takeout double, you are expecting partner to choose a trump suit. If you win the auction, your hand will then be put down on the table as the dummy. This affects your thinking when valuing your hand.

HIGH-CARD STRENGTH

High cards are valued in the same manner as opening the bidding: 4 points for an Ace, 3 points for a King, 2 points for a Queen, and 1 point for a Jack.

DISTRIBUTION

Valuing distribution for a takeout double can be more controversial. Players might use comments such as "I struck gold with this hand," or "I fell in love with my hand." What they are generally referring to is the value of shortness in the opponent's suit. A straightforward way to value distribution is to use *dummy points*, since you're planning to be the dummy: 5 points for a *void*, 3 points for a *singleton*, and 1 point for a *doubleton*.[1]

Support for the Unbid Suits

Ideally, the doubler should have four-card or longer support for the unbid suits, leaving a singleton or void in the opponent's suit. In practice, you won't be making enough use of the takeout double if you wait for the ideal distribution. Three-card support for one of the unbid suits . . . or for two of the unbid suits if you are really stretching and have some extra strength . . . is generally enough.

With a choice between a four-card major and a four or five-card minor suit, partner will prefer bidding the major suit in response to your takeout double. With a borderline hand, therefore it is more important to have four-card support for an unbid major than an unbid minor suit. The more strength you have, the more you can afford to deviate from the ideal distribution. Extra high cards compensate for the lack of support in one of the unbid suits.

Other Considerations

Once you have valued your hand, consider the *level* and the *vulnerability*.

LEVEL

If the player on your right opens the bidding 1♣, and you make a takeout double and the next opponent passes, partner will be able to bid at the one level . . . 1♦, 1♥, or 1♠. If the opening bid is 1♠ partner will be forced to choose a suit at the two level. If the opening bid is 2♠, a takeout double will force your partner to bid a suit at the three level. The higher the level, the more you require. There is no guarantee that partner has any strength at all, so you must have enough to be willing to commit the partnership to compete at the appropriate level.

---

[1] Some experts prefer a less aggressive valuation. For example: 2 points for a void, 1 point for a singleton, 0 points for a doubleton.

The level at which you are forcing partner to bid isn't always clear cut. If the opening bid is 1♥, partner will be able to bid spades at the one level but will have to go to the two level to bid clubs or diamonds.

VULNERABILITY

Any competitive action runs the risk of getting the partnership too high and being doubled for penalties by the opponents. Be cautious when you are vulnerable and the opponents are not. When you are non vulnerable and the opponents are vulnerable, you can afford to be aggressive since the opponents won't be satisfied collecting a small penalty if they think they can make a game or a slam. At equal vulnerability . . . both sides non vulnerable or both sides vulnerable . . . take the middle road, not too cautious nor too aggressive.[2]

Examples

You are sitting South. What is your call in the following auction?

West	North	East	South
		1♦	?

♠ A Q J 5
♥ J 9 6 4
♦ 9 3
♣ A Q 6

Double. This hand qualifies for a takeout double with 14 high-card points and 1 point for distribution, the doubleton diamond. It has acceptable shape with four-card support for hearts and spades, and reasonable three-card support if partner chooses clubs.

♠ A J 10 8
♥ Q 8 7 6 3
♦ —
♣ K 9 4 3

Double. There are only 10 high-card points but the diamond void can be counted as 5 dummy points, giving a total of 15 points. You expect to play the hand in a suit contract other than

[2] Vunerability is only a consideration with a borderline decision. In most cases, it can be ignored.

diamonds with partner as the declarer. The double is more flexible than 1♥. The partnership could find a fit in any of the three unbid suits.

♠ Q 7 6 4
♥ 8
♦ A K 6 3
♣ K J 4 2

Pass. A double would show support for the unbid suits and partner might respond in hearts. The hand is unsuitable for a takeout double and there is no good suit to overcall. Pass. You don't have to bid just because you have 13 points.

♠ A K 9 8 4
♥ K 10 3
♦ 6
♣ Q 10 8 6

1♠. You have a definite preference for the spade suit. A takeout double asks partner to pick the suit.

You are sitting South. What is your call in the following auction?

West	North	East	South
		3♥	?

NORTH
WEST — EAST
SOUTH

♠ K J 10 7
♥ 7
♦ A 10 4 2
♣ K Q 9 5

Double. With 13 high-card points plus 3 dummy points for the singleton, you have more than a minimum. Whichever suit partner chooses, you expect an eight-card fit.

♠ K J 10 7
♥ 8 7 3
♦ A 4 2
♣ K Q 5

Pass. The same number of high-card points as the previous example but this hand doesn't have the strength or shape to start competing at the three or four level. If you were to double and partner had to bid 4♦ or 4♣ on a four-card suit with a weak hand, the partnership could be too high.

The Takeout Double After
Left-hand Opponent Opens

The takeout double can be used when your left-hand opponent has opened the bidding and partner passes. You are sitting in the South position after West opens the bidding, North passes, and East bids.

WEST	NORTH	EAST	SOUTH
1♥	PASS	2♥	?

♠ A J 9 5
♥ 6
♦ K Q 6 2
♣ A 10 7 3

Double. This is a standard takeout double for the unbid suits: clubs, diamonds, and spades. You would like to compete at the two level . . . or the three level if partner chooses a minor.

WEST	NORTH	EAST	SOUTH
1♦	PASS	1NT	?

♠ K 10 7 2
♥ A J 8 3
♦ 9 4
♣ K Q 5

Double. This is also a takeout double for the unbid suits: clubs, hearts, and spades. You would have made a double of 1♦ if the opening bid was on your right and there is no need to be deterred by the 1NT response. East could have as few as 6 points, leaving plenty of room for partner to hold some strength.

WEST	NORTH	EAST	SOUTH
1♠	PASS	2♦	?

♠ A 6
♥ K Q 10 5
♦ 6 4
♣ K Q 9 8 3

Double. This is a takeout double for the unbid suits. This time, there are only two unbid suits: clubs and hearts. You are asking partner to choose one of them and you are showing a willingness to compete at the two or three level. Double is more flexible than overcalling 3♣.

The Takeout Double
to Show a Strong Overcall

When an opponent opens the bidding, there are two standard ways to compete. You can make a simple overcall suggesting a trump suit or notrump, or you can use a takeout double to ask partner to choose the suit. A simple overcall has a range of about 7–17 points[3], depending on the level and vulnerability. It is not forcing and partner could pass with as many as 8 or more points with no support for the overcalled suit. An overcall of 1NT shows about 15–18 points. A takeout double has a range starting at about 13 points with no upper limit. You are asking partner to bid something, so it is forcing in the sense that you will get another opportunity to bid.

This difference allows you to use the takeout double to handle hands too strong for a simple overcall. In the past, such hands were shown using a strong jump overcall or a cuebid of the opponent's suit. The modern style is to assign other conventional meanings to jump overcalls and cuebids.

With a hand too strong for a simple overcall:

- Start with a takeout double
- Bid again at the next opportunity to describe the true nature of the hand.

You are sitting South and East opens the bidding 1♥.

WEST	NORTH	EAST	SOUTH
		1♥	?

♠ A K J 9 7 6
♥ A 3
♦ 6 5
♣ K Q J

Double. With 18 high-card points plus 2 length points for the six-card suit, this hand is too strong for a simple overcall of 1♠. Partner might pass with 5 or 6 points and a game could be missed. Instead, start with a takeout double. Partner

---

[3] Some experts recommend an even higher upper range for an overcall.

will assume that you have the classic hand for a
takeout double and will choose one of the unbid
suits, by bidding 2♦ for example. You will now
clarify the nature of the hand by bidding 2♠,
showing a hand too strong for an overcall of 1♠.

♠ K 5
♥ A K J
♦ A 10 7 3
♣ K J 5 2

Double. With 19 high-card points, the hand is
too strong for a simple overcall of 1NT, which
would show a balanced hand of about 15–18
points. Start with a takeout double. If partner
responds 1♠, for example, rebid 1NT . . . showing a hand stronger than a 1NT overcall, about
19–21 points.

The concept of starting with a takeout double to show a hand
too strong to make a simple overcall falls in line with the idea that
the stronger your hand, the less critical it is to have support for all
the unbid suits. If you are strong enough to double and bid again,
you don't need support for everything partner might bid.

Takeout or Penalty?

Even an experienced partnership needs to know whether a double
is for takeout or for penalty. There can be doubles of low-level
contracts that are meant for penalty and doubles of high-level contracts that are meant for takeout. It is best for the partnership to
have some general agreements that cover most situations.

The suggested agreement is to treat all doubles for takeout except
those that the partnership specifically agrees are for penalty. There
are two situations when a double is usually agreed to be for penalty:

1. Doubles of high-level contracts are for penalty.

The precise level at which doubles turn from takeout to penalty is
open to debate. One standard agreement is that doubles of natural

suit bids through the level of 4♥ are for takeout; doubles of 4♠ or higher are for penalty.

Whatever the partnership agreement, the higher the level the more likely the partner of the doubler will consider converting an intended takeout double into a penalty double by passing. If the opponents are at the four level, for example, it may be easier to take four or five tricks on defense than ten or eleven tricks on offense unless the doubler's partner has a very distributional hand.

2. A double of an opening notrump bid is for penalty.

When an opponent opens with a notrump bid, you would need a balanced hand to have support for all four unbid suits and you would be unlikely to have four-card support for the suit partner chooses. Since the notrump opener has a strong hand, it would be dangerous to compete on that basis. Instead, a double traditionally shows a hand that is as strong as the opening notrump bid, or stronger, and partner is expected to leave the double in for penalties except with a very distributional hand.

A successful penalty double of a notrump opening bid is rare, so many partnerships prefer to assign a conventional meaning to the double. Without such an agreement, however, the double is for penalty.

Improving Your Judgment

The takeout double is a powerful tool that provides scope for judgment. Here are tips to help expand the use of the call.

1. Double or Overcall?

When the opponents open the bidding, there are two ways to compete . . . a takeout double or an overcall. Sometimes, you have a choice. Select the action most likely to get partner's cooperation in reaching the best contract. Compare these two hands for South after the auction begins:

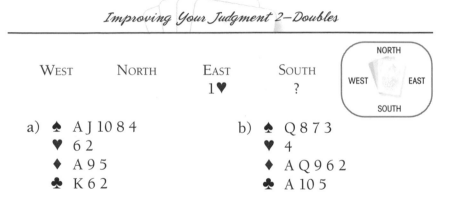

WEST	NORTH	EAST	SOUTH
		1♥	?

a) ♠ A J 10 8 4
   ♥ 6 2
   ♦ A 9 5
   ♣ K 6 2

b) ♠ Q 8 7 3
   ♥ 4
   ♦ A Q 9 6 2
   ♣ A 10 5

With the first hand, an overcall of 1♠ is likely to work better. A double could miss a spade fit unless partner has four or more spades . . . and you might land in a 4-3 fit in a minor suit. Overcalling 1♠ emphasizes the good five-card suit and partner can raise with three-card support. If partner has a five-card or longer minor suit, there's still room to find the fit if partner can't support spades.

With the second hand, a takeout double should work better than an overcall. Overcalling 2♦ leaves less room to find a fit in another suit if partner doesn't like diamonds and it might be costly to miss a 4-4 fit in spades. Doubling will occasionally get you to a 4-3 fit in clubs instead of a better fit in diamonds, but that's the only downside.

2. Watch Out for Wasted Values

The more the strength is concentrated in the unbid suits, the more suitable the hand is for a takeout double. Compare these two hands for South after the auction begins:

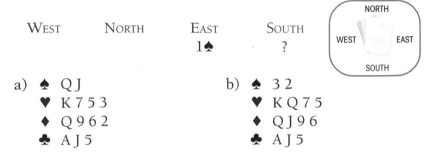

WEST	NORTH	EAST	SOUTH
		1♣	?

a) ♠ Q J
   ♥ K 7 5 3
   ♦ Q 9 6 2
   ♣ A J 5

b) ♠ 3 2
   ♥ K Q 7 5
   ♦ Q J 9 6
   ♣ A J 5

Both hands have 13 high-card points but the second hand is preferable for a takeout double. The first hand has *wasted* strength in the opponent's suit. The ♠Q and ♠J are unlikely to be of much value if your side gets to play the contract. They would be more suitable for defense. In the second hand, there is no wasted strength in spades. The high cards are better placed for whichever trump suit partner chooses.

3. Logically Penalty

On some hands the logic of the auction indicates that a double is meant for penalty, not takeout.

West	North	East	South
		1♥	Pass
2♥	Pass	4♥	Double

In this auction, South's double is for penalty, even if the partnership's general agreement is that doubles are for takeout through the level of 4♥. If South wanted to make a takeout double of hearts, showing the unbid suits, South would have doubled at the first opportunity and not waited until the opponents reached the game level. South might have a hand like this:

♠ A 3
♥ Q J 10 8
♦ A Q 9
♣ 10 8 6 5

4. Over or Under?

Your position at the table can make a difference when you are deciding whether to leave in partner's double or take it out. Compare these two sequences:

a)

WEST	NORTH	EAST	SOUTH
4♣	DOUBLE	PASS	?

```
        NORTH
WEST            EAST
        SOUTH
```

b)

WEST	NORTH	EAST	SOUTH
		1♣	PASS
4♠	DOUBLE	PASS	?

If the partnership agreement is that a double of 4♠ or higher is for penalty, there's still a significant difference between these auctions. In the first auction, North is sitting over the 4♠ bidder and is well placed to make a penalty double. North could easily have something like ♠A-Q-10 and a couple of other high cards[4]. South should only remove the double with a very distributional hand.

In the second auction, North is unlikely to have a strong holding in the spade suit. The opponents have shown a fit and North is not well placed to take tricks in the spade suit. Even a holding such as ♠A-Q-10 may take only one spade trick since the opening bidder is on North's left and may hold both the ♠K and ♠J to trap the ♠Q and ♠10. Instead, North's double is likely based on high cards in the other three suits. That makes it more reasonable for South to take out the double with an unbalanced hand.

---

[4] Most experts play the double of 4♠ to show convertible values . . . enough to defeat 4♠ but also support for the unbid suits in case partner takes out the double with a distributional hand. It is usually best to pass holding length and strength in spades, settling for a small plus score or hoping partner will be able to double.

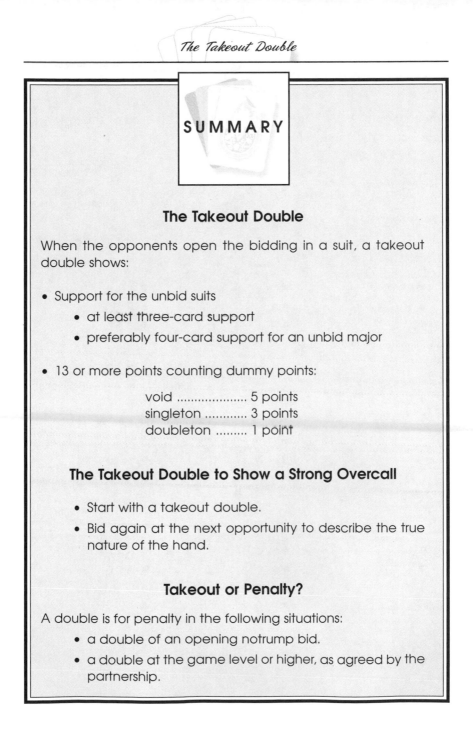

SUMMARY

The Takeout Double

When the opponents open the bidding in a suit, a takeout double shows:

- Support for the unbid suits
  - at least three-card support
  - preferably four-card support for an unbid major

- 13 or more points counting dummy points:

  > void .... 5 points
  > singleton .... 3 points
  > doubleton .... 1 point

The Takeout Double to Show a Strong Overcall

- Start with a takeout double.
- Bid again at the next opportunity to describe the true nature of the hand.

Takeout or Penalty?

A double is for penalty in the following situations:
- a double of an opening notrump bid.
- a double at the game level or higher, as agreed by the partnership.

Quiz – Part I

You are South. What call would you make with each of the following hands after the auction begins:

WEST	NORTH	EAST	SOUTH
		1♣	?

a) ♠ A J 7 5
♥ Q 10 9 3
♦ K 8 4 2
♣ 9

b) ♠ K 10 8 4
♥ A J 5
♦ Q J 7 3
♣ K 6

c) ♠ A K J 7 3
♥ J 8 4
♦ K 5 2
♣ 8 5

d) ♠ A K 6 2
♥ K Q J 9 7 3
♦ 2
♣ A 4

WEST	NORTH	EAST	SOUTH
		1♠	?

e) ♠ —
♥ K J 7 5
♦ A 9 8 6 3
♣ K 6 4 2

f) ♠ A 10 7 3
♥ 9 4
♦ K Q 7 3
♣ A 9 5

g) ♠ K Q 10
♥ A 10 9 3
♦ A K Q 9
♣ J 8

h) ♠ Q 2
♥ Q 5 2
♦ K 7 4 2
♣ A J 5 4

Answers to Quiz – Part I

a) **Double**. There are only 10 high-card points but you can add 3 dummy points for the singleton club. With the ideal distribution for a takeout double it's worth competing, even though your side is vulnerable. Partner will be able to choose a suit at the one level.

b) **Double**. The shape isn't ideal with only three-card support for hearts, but the extra strength in high cards should be enough compensation.

c) **1♠**. You do have support for the unbid suits but, with such a concentration of length and strength in the spade suit, an overcall is more descriptive than a takeout double.

d) **Double**. You don't have support for diamonds, but the hand is too strong for a simple overcall of 1♥. If partner bids diamonds, you intend to bid hearts, showing a strong hand with hearts.

e) **Double**. 11 high-card points plus 5 dummy points for the spade void is more than enough for a takeout double, even though partner will have to choose a suit at the two level.

f) **Pass**. Without support for hearts it would be too risky to make a takeout double on this hand. You don't have to bid just because you hold 13 or more points. You may get another chance to bid later in the auction.

g) **Double**. There is no upper limit to the strength for a takeout double. Despite the inadequate support for clubs, you are strong enough to bid notrump if partner chooses clubs. That shows a hand too strong to overcall 1NT.

h) **Pass**. You have support for the unbid suits and have 12 high-card points plus 1 dummy point for the doubleton spade. Nonetheless, you must exercise some judgment. The ♠Q is unlikely to be worth much, partner would be forced to bid at the two level, and you have only three-card support for hearts . . . the suit partner is most likely to bid with a choice of four-card suits.

Quiz – Part II

You are South. What call would you make with each of the following hands after the auction begins:

WEST	NORTH	EAST	SOUTH
		3♥	?

NORTH

WEST   EAST

SOUTH

a) ♠ Q 10 9 5
   ♥ 6
   ♦ A K 8 3
   ♣ A J 8 5

b) ♠ J 7 5
   ♥ K Q J 9
   ♦ A K
   ♣ 10 9 7 2

c) ♠ A J 4
   ♥ K 4
   ♦ J 7 5
   ♣ A K Q J 6

d) ♠ A K J 2
   ♥ 7 3
   ♦ A 10 6 4 2
   ♣ K 6

WEST	NORTH	EAST	SOUTH
1♠	PASS	2♣	?

NORTH

WEST   EAST

SOUTH

e) ♠ 9 5
   ♥ A J 10 6
   ♦ A K J 4 2
   ♣ 8 6

f) ♠ A 6
   ♥ A Q J 10 8
   ♦ J 8 4 3
   ♣ 7 2

g) ♠ K J 4
   ♥ K 8 4
   ♦ A 6 3
   ♣ Q J 7 2

h) ♠ 4
   ♥ K J 7 5 3
   ♦ A Q 8 4 2
   ♣ 9 5

Answers to Quiz – Part II

a) **Double**. Although partner will have to bid at the three or four level, your excellent support for the unbid suits and your strength—14 high-card points plus 3 points for the singleton heart-should be enough to compete.

b) **Pass**. A double would be for takeout, not for penalty. Partner still has an opportunity to bid. If partner doubles, you can pass and collect a large penalty.

c) **3NT**. You could double, but that is likely to get the partnership beyond the most likely game contract for your side . . . 3NT. Better to overcall 3NT and hope partner has a couple of useful high cards. You can expect partner to hold at least 6 or 7 points when an opponent preempts.

d) **Double**. Tough hand. Too much to pass but overcalling 4♦ could land you in a poor spot. Double will work well if partner bids spades or diamonds. If partner bids clubs, you might feel un-comfortable putting down the dummy.

e) **Double**. This shows support for the unbid suits, diamonds and hearts, and willingness to compete at the two level or higher. If you overcall 2♦, a heart fit might get lost.

f) **2♥**. Although you could double to show both hearts and diamonds, this hand is more heart-oriented. It's probably best to emphasize the hearts with an overcall and forget about the diamonds.

g) **Pass**. You have some high cards but only three-card support for the unbid suits. Best to keep quiet and keep out of trouble.

h) **Double**. Not too much in the way of high cards but you definitely want to suggest competing in hearts or diamonds.

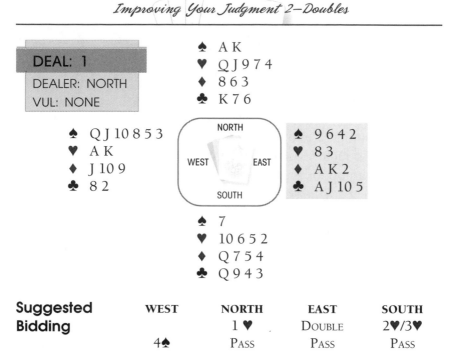

DEAL: 1

DEALER: NORTH
VUL: NONE

NORTH
♠ A K
♥ Q J 9 7 4
♦ 8 6 3
♣ K 7 6

WEST
♠ Q J 10 8 5 3
♥ A K
♦ J 10 9
♣ 8 2

EAST
♠ 9 6 4 2
♥ 8 3
♦ A K 2
♣ A J 10 5

SOUTH
♠ 7
♥ 10 6 5 2
♦ Q 7 5 4
♣ Q 9 4 3

Suggested Bidding

WEST	NORTH	EAST	SOUTH
	1 ♥	DOUBLE	2♥/3♥
4♠	PASS	PASS	PASS

North opens the bidding at the one level with 13 high-card points plus 1 length point for the five-card suit. East can make a takeout double with support for the unbid suits and 12 high-card points plus 1 dummy point for the doubleton heart.

South has 4 high-card points and 3 dummy points for the singleton spade, enough to raise to the two level. The popular modern style, however, is to use *preemptive jump raises* after a takeout double. South could jump to 3♥ in an attempt to make the auction difficult for the opponents. Whatever action South takes, West should bid game in spades. West has 11 high-card points plus 2 length points for the six-card suit. Since partner has promised the values for an opening bid and support for spades, one of the unbid suits, the partnership belongs in game.

Suggested Opening Lead

North is on lead against West's 4♠ contract. With hearts bid and raised by North-South, North should lead the ♥Q, top of the touching high cards from a *broken sequence*.

Suggested Play

Declarer, has two losers in spades, a potential loser in diamonds, and a potential loser in clubs. That's one too many. One possibility to get rid of a loser is to take the diamond finesse, hoping North has the ♦Q. That's a 50% chance. The club suit, however, offers a better option.

By finessing twice in clubs, declarer can develop an extra winner 75% of the time. West's diamond loser could then be discarded on the extra club winner. The repeated club finesse will be successful if North holds the ♣K, or the ♣Q, or both the ♣K and ♣Q. It will fail if South holds both the ♣K and ♣Q. In three of the four possible layouts for the missing club honors, declarer will succeed.

A consideration in a trump contract is when to draw trumps. On this hand, West has to get rid of the diamond loser before drawing trumps. Otherwise, the defenders have a chance to defeat the contract.

After winning the first heart trick, West should lead a club and finesse dummy's ♣J, or ♣10. South will win the ♣Q and can lead another heart. Declarer wins this, and takes a second club finesse. This time, the finesse is successful and declarer can use dummy's ♣A on the third round to discard a diamond loser. Declarer loses two spade tricks and a club trick.

Suggested Defense

The defenders can't defeat the contract if declarer, before drawing trumps, uses the club suit to get rid of the diamond loser. If declarer takes the diamond finesse, South will win the ♦Q and the defenders will later get a club trick to go with the two spade winners.

Declarer can make the contract by using the club suit but it's important to take the club finesse early in the play. Otherwise, the defenders will have an opportunity to defeat the contract.

If North leads the ♥Q, South should make a discouraging signal by playing the ♥2 since South knows declarer holds both the ♥A and ♥K. If declarer leads a trump right away, North can win and, based on South's discouraging signal, switch to a diamond, hoping to establish a trick for the defenders in that suit. If declarer wins and leads a second trump, North can win and lead another diamond. That will establish South's ♦Q as a winner before declarer can establish a second winner in the club suit.

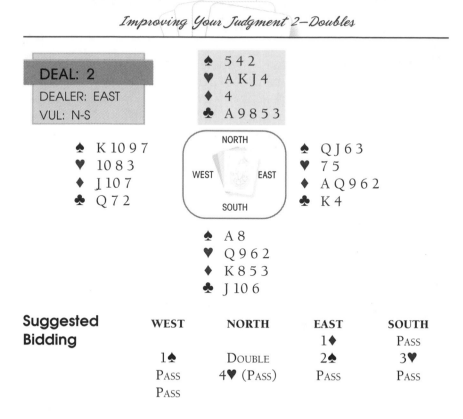

	DEAL: 2	**♠** 5 4 2	
	DEALER: EAST	**♥** A K J 4	
	VUL: N-S	**♦** 4	
		♣ A 9 8 5 3	

♠ K 10 9 7
♥ 10 8 3
♦ J 10 7
♣ Q 7 2

♠ Q J 6 3
♥ 7 5
♦ A Q 9 6 2
♣ K 4

♠ A 8
♥ Q 9 6 2
♦ K 8 5 3
♣ J 10 6

Suggested	WEST	NORTH	EAST	SOUTH
Bidding			1♦	PASS
	1♠	DOUBLE	2♠	3♥
	PASS	4♥ (PASS)	PASS	PASS
	PASS			

East opens 1♦. South doesn't have a suitable hand for entering the auction at this point. West has enough to respond 1♠. North, with support for both hearts and clubs, the unbid suits, can show interest in competing by making a takeout double.

East should make the normal rebid of raising to 2♠. North's double isn't for penalties and East still wants to win the auction if possible. South, with 10 high-card points, has enough to compete even though the auction is now at the three level. Since North has promised at least an opening bid, the partnership has a minimum of 23 combined points and should have at least an eight-card fit in hearts.

West has nothing more to say but North might want to take another bid. North has the top of the minimum range for a takeout double . . . 12 high-card points plus 3 points for the singleton diamond . . . and South's willingness to compete to the three level shows about 9–11 points. It's a close decision, but North might raise South to the game level.

Suggested Opening Lead

Against South's heart contract, West has a choice of leading spades . . . the suit the partnership has bid and raised . . . or diamonds . . . partner's first bid suit. With touching honors in partner's suit, West will likely choose the ♦J.

Suggested Play

Declarer has a spade loser, four diamond losers, and two club losers. After an opening diamond lead, declarer's ♦K will become a winner, eliminating one of the diamond losers. There are still six losers, three too many.

Declarer might think about ruffing two diamond losers in the North hand. That isn't likely to be successful on this hand. Declarer needs at least two of dummy's high hearts to draw trump and declarer will run into entry difficulties getting back to the South hand to lead diamonds for a second time. A better plan is to get rid of two diamond losers on dummy's long club suit.

Suppose East wins the ♦A and switches to the ♠Q. South can win the ♠A and is in the right hand to lead the ♣J or ♣10, taking a finesse when West plays low. East can win the ♣K and the defenders will likely take their spade winner and play a third round of spades. Declarer can ruff and then draw three rounds of trump, ending in the South hand with the ♥Q. With the trumps drawn, declarer can now lead the ♣10. Whether or not West covers with the ♣Q, declarer takes the remaining tricks. South's diamond losers are discarded on North's club winners. Declarer's only losers are one spade, one diamond, and one club.

Suggested Defense

If declarer handles the club suit as described above, the defenders can't prevent North-South from taking ten tricks.

It won't help for West to lead a spade initially. Declarer wins the ♠A, and takes a club finesse. After winning the ♣K, East can take a spade trick and the ♦A, but that's all. Declarer can take the rest of the tricks as before by drawing trumps and repeating the club finesse.

DEAL: 3
DEALER: SOUTH
VUL: E-W

♠ Q J 9
♥ 10 9 7 6
♦ 2
♣ A K Q 8 5

♠ A K 6 2
♥ A K J 4
♦ 9 4
♣ J 7 4

NORTH

WEST   EAST

SOUTH

♠ 8 7 4 3
♥ Q 5 2
♦ A 7 5
♣ 10 3 2

♠ 10 5
♥ 8 3
♦ K Q J 10 8 6 3
♣ 9 6

Suggested Bidding

WEST	NORTH	EAST	SOUTH
			3♦
DOUBLE	PASS	3♠	PASS
PASS	PASS		

South's hand is ideal for an opening *preemptive bid* at the three level with an excellent seven-card diamond suit and no defense in the other suits. West has enough for a takeout double at the three level with 16 high-card points and 1 dummy point for the doubleton diamond. West needs more than a minimum takeout double to bring partner into the auction at the three level or higher, especially when vulnerable.

North has no reason to bid opposite partner's preemptive bid. With no fit for diamonds, 3NT is unlikely to have any real chance and a bid of 4♣ will get the partnership too high. East, with 6 high-card points, doesn't have enough to jump to game opposite partner's takeout double and simply bids spades at the cheapest level.

South has said everything with the 3♦ preempt and West should also pass. West has a nice hand but partner could have very little. West can expect partner to hold about 6 or 7 points when an opponent makes a preemptive opening bid, but that won't be enough for game. West has to trust that East would jump to game opposite a three-level takeout double with about 9 or more points. East's 3♠ call should end the auction.

Suggested Opening Lead

South is on lead against 3♠ and would start with the ♦K, top of the *solid sequence.*

Suggested Play

3♠ is a precarious contract. Even if the missing spades divide 3-2, declarer, has a spade loser. There are two diamond losers and three club losers. Two losers have to be eliminated. One of the diamond losers can be trumped in the dummy. A club loser can be discarded on the extra heart winner in the West hand.

The defenders will take their three club winners if declarer gives up the lead before getting rid of one of the club losers. Declarer also can't afford to play hearts before some of the trumps are drawn, otherwise one of the heart winners might get ruffed.

East's best chance is to win the ♦A and play exactly two rounds of trumps, leaving the high trump outstanding. Now declarer can play hearts, hoping the defender with the remaining trump won't be able to ruff the first three rounds. East doesn't care if the fourth round of hearts is trumped because East is throwing away a club loser and had to lose the high spade anyway. On the actual hand, North has to follow suit to all four rounds of hearts and declarer can discard a club loser from the East hand. Now declarer can give up a diamond trick and, when East gets the lead again, a diamond loser can be ruffed in dummy. Declarer loses one spade, one diamond, and two clubs.

Suggested Defense

South can actually defeat the contract by leading a club at trick one, but that's unlikely. South has a normal opening lead of the ♦K. If South were to lead a club, North would have to take three club winners and lead a fourth round of clubs to defeat the contract[5]. South can then ruff with the ♠10. Whether or not declarer overruffs, the defense then gets two trump tricks. That's a very unlikely defense.

---

[5] If North takes three club winners and leads a diamond, declarer can make the contract. Declarer wins the ♦A, draws two rounds of trumps, and takes the four heart winners, discarding a diamond. Declarer can then lead a spade and North has to lead a club, allowing declarer to discard the remaining diamond loser and trump in dummy.

DEAL: 4

DEALER: WEST
VUL: BOTH

♠ K 7 6 2
♥ J 8 4 3
♦ J 4
♣ K 8 3

NORTH

WEST   EAST

SOUTH

♠ 8 5
♥ 10 9 6
♦ Q 10 9 6
♣ 10 7 5 2

♠ Q J 10 9 3
♥ A K 7
♦ 8
♣ Q J 6 4

♠ A 4
♥ Q 5 2
♦ A K 7 5 3 2
♣ A 9

Suggested Bidding

WEST	NORTH	EAST	SOUTH
PASS	PASS	1♠	DOUBLE
PASS	2♥	PASS	3♦
PASS	3NT	PASS	PASS
PASS			

West and North pass. East opens the bidding 1♠. South, with 17 high-card points plus two length points for the six-card suit, is too strong to overcall 2♦. Instead, South starts with a takeout double. West passes. North, with 8 high-card points and some strength in spades, might choose to bid 1NT but, with a four-card heart suit, 2♥ is more likely to put the partnership in its best fit.

East passes and South describes the true nature of the hand by bidding 3♦. This shows a hand too strong for a simple overcall of 2♦ ... about 17 or more points. North should bid 3NT with 8 points and something in spades. North can reason that it will probably be as easy to take nine tricks in notrump as in diamonds. North's 3NT call should end the auction.

Suggested Opening Lead

Against 3NT, East will lead the ♠Q, top of the solid sequence.

Suggested Play

Declarer, has six top tricks: two spades, two diamonds, and two clubs. The three additional tricks required will likely have to come from the diamond suit. That won't be a problem if the missing diamonds are divided 3-2. Declarer could be unlucky. The diamonds could break 5-0, or 4-1 with East having the four diamonds including the ♦Q. Then there is nothing declarer can do. On the actual hand, West has four diamonds including the ♦Q. Declarer's best plan is to lead toward the ♦J. If West holds the ♦Q, declarer can now take five diamond tricks. Even if East holds the ♦Q, declarer will still get five diamond tricks if the diamonds are divided 3-2.

The only time leading toward the ♦J doesn't work is if East holds the singleton ♦Q . . . in which case playing a high diamond first will work. Since East is more likely to hold the singleton ♦6, ♦8, ♦9, or ♦10 than the singleton ♦Q, the odds are strongly in favor of leading toward the ♦J.

Leading the ♦J will never gain unless East fails to cover holding the ♦Q. Either it will lose to West's ♦Q, or East will cover the ♦J with the ♦Q, promoting one or more tricks for the defenders depending on how the suit breaks.

Having decided to lead toward the ♦J, declarer has to win the first trick with South's ♣A, not North's ♣K. Declarer will then be in the right hand to lead a low diamond toward the ♦J. If West plays low, North's ♦J will win and declarer can then take the ♦A-K and give up a diamond. The ♣A will provide an entry to dummy's established diamonds. If West plays the ♦Q when a low diamond is led from dummy, North plays low. Assuming West returns a spade, North wins, takes the ♦J, and then uses the ♣A as an entry to dummy's diamonds.

Suggested Defense

If declarer doesn't play the hand as described above, the defenders have a chance to defeat the contract. If declarer wins the ♣A and then plays the ♦A and ♦K and leads a third diamond, West wins and returns a spade which is won by North's ♠K. Now, three winners are established for East. On regaining the lead with another diamond, West can lead a heart. East will take the ♥A, ♥K, and remaining spade winners to defeat the contract three tricks.

If you don't plan on responding to your partner's takeout double with no points, be sure to drive to the bridge game in separate cars.

2

Advancing a Takeout Double

The partner of the opening bidder is referred to as the *responder*. A modern term for the player who responds to a takeout double or an overcall is the *advancer*. That's the term that will be used in this book. The diagram illustrates your position at the table after West opens the bidding and your partner, North, makes a takeout double:

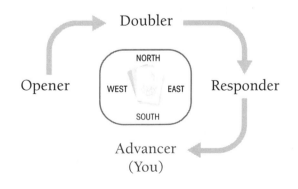

Doubler

NORTH

Opener   WEST   EAST   Responder

SOUTH

Advancer
(You)

The takeout double is *forcing* and, if your right-hand opponent passes, you are expected to bid. The first challenge is to accept this concept, even when it appears as though it will be disastrous. Imagine the worst case scenario. Partner has made a takeout double and the only feature in your hand is a long, weak holding in the opponent's suit. No excuse. Partner is counting on you to choose your best suit.

In today's game, even with a weak hand, right-hand opponent will often bid after partner's takeout double. Advancer is no longer forced to bid, but that shouldn't stop you from competing whenever possible. Partner's takeout double is an invitation to enter the auction and you should be willing to accept if you have enough to compete. Add your strength to 13 and, if you come to a total of 20 or more, you may want to bid.

Be aggressive when you are advancing partner's takeout double. When an opponent has opened the bidding, experts suggest your side can reasonably look for game with only 24 points instead of the usual 25 or 26. Most of the opponents' high cards will be in opener's hand and this will help you on play.

Let's take a closer look at advancing a takeout double to clarify how you and your partner can bid competitively to the best spot.

Advancing the Takeout Double

There are two decisions for advancer after partner makes a takeout double and right-hand opponent passes.

- To pick the suit (or notrump).
- To bid to the appropriate level.

Picking the Suit

Partner has asked you to choose a trump suit and you generally pick the longest suit, since that should be the longest combined suit for the partnership. With a choice of suits, bid the *higher-ranking*.

Bidding at the Appropriate Level

With a weak hand, 0–8 points, bid at the cheapest level; with an *invitational* hand, 9–11 points, jump a level; with 12 or more points, get to game. The point ranges aren't quite the same as responding to an opening bid. You have a wider range to cover for minimum hands (0–8) and you are slightly more aggressive with invitational hands (9–11), but the concept is similar.

ADVANCING A TAKEOUT DOUBLE

0 – 8 points: Bid at the cheapest level.
9 – 11 points: Make an invitational bid by jumping one level.
12+ points: Get the partnership to game.

The level at which you actually bid varies depending on how the auction has gone beforehand. Consider this auction. You are South:

WEST	NORTH	EAST	SOUTH
1♣	DOUBLE	PASS	?

Bidding hearts at the cheapest level would get you to 2♥. Jumping a level to show an invitational hand would get you to 3♥.

Suppose the auction begins like this:

WEST	NORTH	EAST	SOUTH
1♥	DOUBLE	PASS	?

Spades could be bid at the one level with a weak hand. A jump to 2♠ would show an invitational hand. If the best suit is diamonds, you would have to bid 2♦ with a minimum hand and jump to 3♦ with an invitational hand.

Consider this auction:

WEST	NORTH	EAST	SOUTH
		1♠	PASS
2♠	DOUBLE	PASS	?

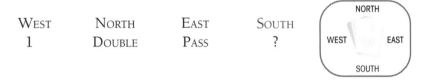

To bid hearts at the cheapest level you have to bid 3♥. Jumping with an invitational hand of 9–11 points will get you to 4♥. Does this make sense? Yes. Partner should have more than a minimum 13 points to make a takeout double that commits the partnership to at least the three level. If partner has a hand worth 15 or 16 points, or more, then you likely belong in game when you have about 9–11 points. You can afford to be more aggressive bidding games when you know where most of the missing points are located. You should land at a reasonable level.

Examples

What call do you make when you are South in the following auction:

WEST	NORTH	EAST	SOUTH
1	DOUBLE	PASS	?

♠ 10 7 6 4 2
♥ 10 8 5
♦ 9 6 3
♣ 8 4

1♠. Since the player on your right didn't bid, you must say something. Even though you have no high cards and can count only 1 point for the five-card spade suit, bid the longest suit at the cheapest level. Partner has promised support for the suit you choose.

♠ 10 6
♥ J 10 7 3
♦ 8 5 2
♣ A Q 6 2

1♥. Although the clubs are stronger than the hearts it's better to show the higher-ranking suit. You can do so at a lower level and major suit contracts are worth more than minor suit contracts.

30

♠ Q 4
♥ 9 6 3
♦ 10 8 2
♣ Q J 8 6 4

2♣. Bid the longest suit at the cheapest level. Although you're bidding a new suit at the two level, you don't need 11 or more points when advancing over a takeout double. Partner has asked you to bid, and the situation is more comparable to raising partner's suit than to introducing a new suit of your own.

♠ A Q 7 4
♥ 6 3
♦ K J 8 6
♣ J 9 3

2♠. With 11 high-card points, the partnership is close to the strength needed for a game contract. The jump sends an invitational message. Partner can pass with minimum values for a takeout double or bid on to game with a little extra.

♠ K 4
♥ J 9 2
♦ 7 3
♣ A Q 10 8 6 4

3♣. With 10 high-card points and a six-card suit, make an invitational bid by jumping a level. Bid 3♣, rather than 2♣. You should be safe at the three level since partner is showing an opening bid with support for the suit you choose. If partner has extra strength, a game contract is in sight.

♠ A 7
♥ Q J 9 6 4 2
♦ Q 6
♣ Q 10 4

4♥. With 11 high-card points and a six-card suit, you have enough to be in game opposite partner's takeout double. Even if partner has only three-card support for hearts, 4♥ should be an excellent contract.

What call do you make as South in the following auction:

WEST	NORTH	EAST	SOUTH
		1♠	PASS
2♦	DOUBLE	PASS	?

NORTH

WEST   EAST

SOUTH

♠ 6 5 3
♥ 8
♦ Q 8 5 2
♣ J 9 7 5 2

3♣. Partner is asking you to pick one of the unbid suits, hearts or clubs. With a weak hand, bid at the cheapest level. That gets you to the three level, but partner should have better than a minimum takeout double to bring the partnership into the auction when the opponents are already at the two level.

♠ J 5
♥ K Q 8 7
♦ A 6 5 2
♣ 10 7 2

3♥. With 10 high-card points, there is enough for an invitational bid. Jump to the three level, since 2♥ would show 0-8 points. The jump is similar to making a limit raise if partner opened the bidding 1♥. Partner can pass with a minimum for the takeout double.

♠ A K 3
♥ 9 7 6 4 2
♦ 10 8 2
♣ K Q

4♥. With an opening bid opposite partner's opening bid, get the partnership to game. Don't worry about the quality of the heart suit. Partner should have at least three-card support.

♠ J 8 2
♥ Q 8 6
♦ 10 7 4 3
♣ 6 5 4

2♥. An unattractive choice. You have to say something and you can't bid notrump with so little strength in the opponents' suits. You have to manufacture a bid on a three-card suit.

Bidding Notrump

The doubler has described a hand that is short in the suit bid by your opponent. Playing in one of the unbid suits is the first priority, even when advancer has some strength in the opponent's suit. Your high cards in the suit are poorly placed when the opening bidder is on your left. On the other hand, if you have a reasonable amount of strength, it's likely that your right-hand opponent has a very weak hand because both opener and partner have 13 or more points. Now it will be difficult for your right-hand opponent to gain the lead to trap honors you hold in left-hand opponent's suit. Bidding notrump becomes a more viable option.

If you decide that notrump is the best choice:[6]

ADVANCING IN NOTRUMP

With good cards in the opponent's suit and no better option, bid notrump using the following ranges:

6 – 10 points:	Bid notrump at the cheapest level.
11 – 12 points:	Bid notrump, jumping a level.
13+ points:	Bid game in notrump.

Example

What do you make as South in the following auction:

WEST	NORTH	EAST	SOUTH
1♦	DOUBLE	PASS	?

♠ 9 7 2
♥ Q 8 6
♦ A J 9 8
♣ Q 10 4

1NT. With no four-card suit to bid, and with most of the strength in the opponent's suit, bid 1NT. You should have some length and strength in left-hand opponent's suit before considering notrump. Partner has made a takeout double and is unlikely to have many diamonds.

[6] Some experts suggest slightly stronger ranges when advancing in notrump opposite partner's assumed shortness. For example: 1NT = 7–11; 2NT = 12–14; 3NT = 15 or more.

Advancer's Cuebid

At times, advancer, with a game-going or invitational hand, needs more information from the doubler before deciding the best contract. Bidding or jumping in one of the unbid suits is not forcing, so advancer needs a forcing call. There's one bid readily available for that purpose . . . a bid of the opponent's suit at the cheapest level. A bid of the opponent's suit by advancer is called a *cuebid*. After partner's takeout double, you can't want to play in the opponent's suit. With enough length and strength in their suit to want to play with that suit as trump, pass partner's takeout double and choose to defend.

A cuebid of the opponent's suit in a competitive auction is simply an artificial forcing bid, asking for additional information from partner to help reach the best contract. You are South in the following auction:

WEST	NORTH	EAST	SOUTH
1♣	DOUBLE	PASS	?

NORTH

WEST — EAST

SOUTH

♠ A 10 9 4
♥ A J 6 4
♦ 10 8 3
♣ A 7

2♣. You want to be in game after partner's takeout double, but it's unclear whether 4♥ or 4♠ is better. You could pick one of the suits and bid game, but it won't hurt to get more information from partner who might have doubled with three cards in one of the major suits. Make a forcing bid by cuebidding 2♣. This has nothing to do with the club suit.

After hearing partner's next bid, advancer is better placed to decide the best contract. If partner bids 2♥, promising at least a four-card heart suit, raise to 4♥. If partner bids 2♠, raise to 4♠. If partner bids 2♦ . . . presumably because partner doesn't have four hearts or four spades . . . get to game in diamonds or try 3NT. If you're still uncertain what to do after hearing partner's rebid, you can always cuebid again.

Advancer's cuebid shows a hand of at least invitational strength and is forcing until a trump suit has been agreed. After a cuebid. the bid of a new suit or notrump by advancer below the game level is forcing. If advancer cuebids and then raises partner's suit, it is invitational. You hold the following hand as South with the same auction:

♠ K 10 9 4
♥ Q J 6 4
♦ 10 8 3
♣ A 7

2♣. Over partner's takeout double of 1♣, it's unclear whether to jump to 2♥ or 2♠ as an invitational bid. Instead, start with a cuebid of 2♣. If partner bids 2♥, raise to 3♥. If partner bids 2♠, raise to 3♠.

When Responder Bids
Over the Takeout Double

Although partner's takeout double is a request for you, the advancer, to bid, if your right-hand opponent, responder, makes a call, you could now pass. Consider the following auction as South:

WEST	NORTH	EAST	SOUTH
1♥	DOUBLE	2♥	?

If East passed, you would have to bid something. When East bids, you could pass because partner has another chance to bid. Just because you can pass doesn't mean that you should pass. Consider these two hands:

1) ♠ 9 6 4
   ♥ Q 7 2
   ♦ J 8 5 4
   ♣ 9 7 3

2) ♠ K J 7 3
   ♥ 8 5 2
   ♦ K 9 6 4
   ♣ 10 7

With the first hand, you are happy to be given the opportunity to pass. With the second hand, however, bid 2♠ to compete for the contract, even though you could pass. Partner invited you into the auction and has at least 13 points and support for spades. Since you have 7 points, the partnership is likely to have as much strength as the opponents. Don't let them play in their best trump suit when you have a reasonable alternative. By bidding without jumping you are only showing about 6-8 points. With less, you would pass; with more, you would make an invitational bid by jumping to 3♠.

Consider the following auction where there is a *redouble* and you are sitting South:

WEST	NORTH	EAST	SOUTH
1♥	DOUBLE	REDOUBLE	?

Again, because East has bid, South could pass. In this auction, partner doesn't expect you to have a very good hand. West has 13 or more points for the opening bid; North has 13 or more for the takeout double; East has 10 or more for the redouble. You should, however, consider bidding with a preference for one of the unbid suits. North-South is trying to escape as cheaply as possible to the best spot. Compare these two hands in the above auction:

1) ♠ 9 6 4
 ♥ J 8
 ♦ 10 8 7 3
 ♣ 9 7 6 3

2) ♠ 7 3
 ♥ 9 8 5 2
 ♦ 6 4
 ♣ Q J 9 7 5

With the first hand, you don't have a clear-cut preference. You would have to go to the two level to bid one of the minor suits and have no reason to choose one over the other. Pass and let partner pick the suit. With the second hand, there is a clear-cut preference for clubs. Bid 2♣. If you pass, partner might choose to bid 2♦ and you won't be able to bid clubs without going to the three level.

Improving Your Judgment

1. Advancer's Duplicated Values

Advancer values the hand aggressively. Having said that, avoid *duplicating values* that partner is already counting. Unless you are planning to bid notrump, a stray king, queen, or jack in the opponent's suit is likely to be wasted opposite partner's assumed shortness. Your shortness in an unbid suit may be facing partner's high cards in that suit, so use a slightly more conservative scale to count shortness: 3 points for a void; 2 for a singleton; 1 for a doubleton. Compare these two hands for South in the following auction:

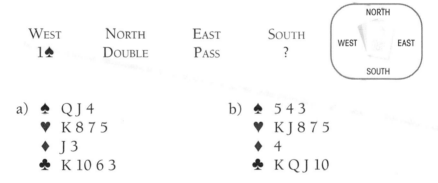

WEST	NORTH	EAST	SOUTH
1♣	DOUBLE	PASS	?

a) ♠ Q J 4
    ♥ K 8 7 5
    ♦ J 3
    ♣ K 10 6 3

b) ♠ 5 4 3
    ♥ K J 8 7 5
    ♦ 4
    ♣ K Q J 10

With the first hand, your ♠Q and ♠J in the opponent's suit may not be worth much opposite partner's likely shortness. Despite the 10 high-card points, this hand is barely worth an invitational jump to 3♥ and some players would be content to treat it as a minimum and bid only 2♥. The second hand also has 10 high-card points but is probably worth a jump right to 4♥. There's nothing wasted in spades. Your high cards are working well together. Give yourself a length point for the fifth heart and 2 points for the singleton diamond . . . enough to try for a game!

2. Preferring the Major Suit

Although you generally bid the longer suit when advancing over a takeout double, playing in a major can take precedence. Consider this hand after the auction begins:

WEST	NORTH	EAST	SOUTH
1♠	DOUBLE	3♠	?

♠ 4
♥ Q 10 8 7
♦ K 4
♣ A J 8 7 5 4

Bidding 4♣ would be safe, but it doesn't get you a game bonus. If you're going to try for ten tricks, bid 4♥. There should be an eight-card fit in hearts, enough to have a chance at game.

3. Converting Partner's Takeout Double into a Penalty Double

When partner makes a takeout double you can pass, converting the double into a penalty double. This should be done rarely. It isn't enough to have length in the opponent's suit, especially at a low level. You need a solid holding, such as Q-J-10-9-3-2 because you want to successfully draw trumps. Lead trumps as often as possible when defending a low-level doubled contract. By drawing the opponents' trumps, your side's high cards can take tricks. Compare these two hands in the following auction:

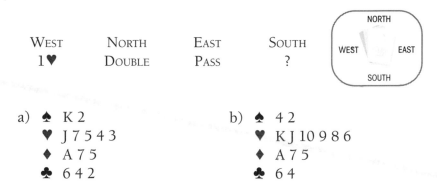

WEST	NORTH	EAST	SOUTH
1♥	DOUBLE	PASS	?

a) ♠ K 2
   ♥ J 7 5 4 3
   ♦ A 7 5
   ♣ 6 4 2

b) ♠ 4 2
   ♥ K J 10 9 8 6
   ♦ A 7 5
   ♣ 6 4

With the first hand, bid. 1NT is much better than pass. You may not take a single trick in hearts, despite your length. On the second hand, you can afford to pass, expecting to take four trump tricks to go with the ♦A. Partner's high cards should provide enough to defeat the contract.

4. The Responsive Double

If responder raises opener's suit to the two or three level over the takeout double, many partnerships play that a double by advancer is for takeout rather than penalty. This is called a *responsive double* and the partnership can agree to use this convention. Consider this hand after the auction begins:

WEST	NORTH	EAST	SOUTH
1♦	DOUBLE	3♦	?

♠ K J 7 5
♥ A J 8 2
♦ 8 7
♣ J 6 3

There is enough to compete at the three level but you don't want to pick the wrong suit. You can't afford to cuebid 4♦ because that would commit the partnership to the game level. The responsive double solves the dilemma. Let partner pick the suit.

The responsive double shows:[7]

- Both major suits if the opponents are bidding and raising a minor suit. With just one major, bid it.

- Both minor suits if the opponents are bidding and raising a major suit. With the unbid major suit or if the only suit is a minor, you would bid that suit.

---

[7] The responsive double is complex and there are many possible agreements. This is a simplified explanation.

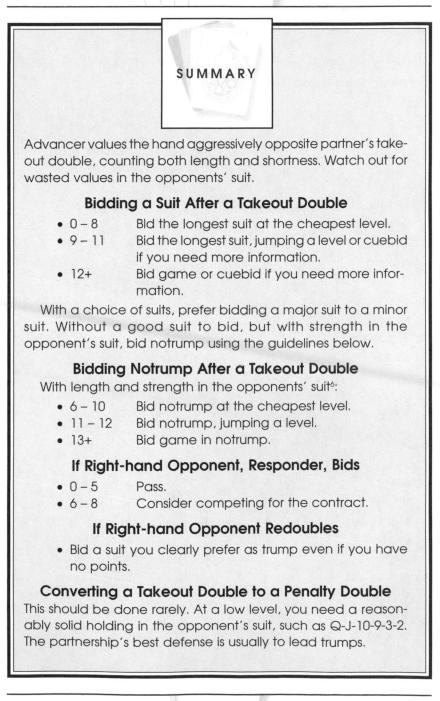

SUMMARY

Advancer values the hand aggressively opposite partner's take-out double, counting both length and shortness. Watch out for wasted values in the opponents' suit.

Bidding a Suit After a Takeout Double

- 0 – 8   Bid the longest suit at the cheapest level.
- 9 – 11   Bid the longest suit, jumping a level or cuebid if you need more information.
- 12+   Bid game or cuebid if you need more information.

With a choice of suits, prefer bidding a major suit to a minor suit. Without a good suit to bid, but with strength in the opponent's suit, bid notrump using the guidelines below.

Bidding Notrump After a Takeout Double

With length and strength in the opponents' suit[6]:

- 6 – 10   Bid notrump at the cheapest level.
- 11 – 12   Bid notrump, jumping a level.
- 13+   Bid game in notrump.

If Right-hand Opponent, Responder, Bids

- 0 – 5   Pass.
- 6 – 8   Consider competing for the contract.

If Right-hand Opponent Redoubles

- Bid a suit you clearly prefer as trump even if you have no points.

Converting a Takeout Double to a Penalty Double

This should be done rarely. At a low level, you need a reasonably solid holding in the opponent's suit, such as Q-J-10-9-3-2. The partnership's best defense is usually to lead trumps.

Quiz – Part I

You are South. What call would you make with each of the following hands after the auction begins:

WEST	NORTH	EAST	SOUTH
1♥	DOUBLE	PASS	?

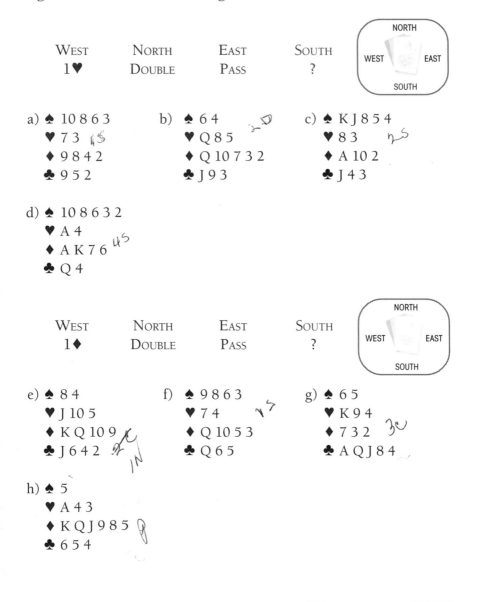

a) ♠ 10 8 6 3
♥ 7 3
♦ 9 8 4 2
♣ 9 5 2

b) ♠ 6 4
♥ Q 8 5
♦ Q 10 7 3 2
♣ J 9 3

c) ♠ K J 8 5 4
♥ 8 3
♦ A 10 2
♣ J 4 3

d) ♠ 10 8 6 3 2
♥ A 4
♦ A K 7 6
♣ Q 4

WEST	NORTH	EAST	SOUTH
1♦	DOUBLE	PASS	?

e) ♠ 8 4
♥ J 10 5
♦ K Q 10 9
♣ J 6 4 2

f) ♠ 9 8 6 3
♥ 7 4
♦ Q 10 5 3
♣ Q 6 5

g) ♠ 6 5
♥ K 9 4
♦ 7 3 2
♣ A Q J 8 4

h) ♠ 5
♥ A 4 3
♦ K Q J 9 8 5
♣ 6 5 4

Answers to Quiz – Part I

a) **1♠**. Partner asked you to pick one of the unbid suits. You have to bid something, even with no points. At least you can bid spades at the one level.

b) **2♦**. You still don't have much but your best suit is diamonds so bid it at the cheapest level.

c) **2♠**. With 9 high-card points plus a five-card suit, you have enough to make an invitational bid by jumping a level. This is not forcing. Partner can pass with a minimum takeout double.

d) **4♠**. Don't be concerned with the quality of the spade suit. Partner has promised support so spades will be adequate even if partner only has three-card support. With 13 high-card points and a five-card suit, you have enough to want to be in game opposite partner's promised opening bid.

e) **1NT**. You don't usually bid notrump in response to partner's takeout double but with this hand your strong holding in the opponent's suit suggests that notrump will be a better contract than your alternative choice, 2♣.

f) **1♠**. Although you have some strength in diamonds, you don't have enough to suggest playing in notrump. Besides, bidding notrump would tend to deny a four-card major suit.

g) **3♣**. With 10 high-card points and a five-card suit, you have enough to make an invitational bid. Jumping in your suit gets you to the three level, but that should be fine opposite partner's opening bid and support for the unbid suits.

h) **Pass**. This is the exception to the rule about taking out partner's takeout double. Diamonds is probably the best trump suit for your side since you likely have better diamonds than West.

Quiz – Part II

You are South. What call would you make with each of the following hands after the auction begins:

WEST	NORTH	EAST	SOUTH
1♥	DOUBLE	1NT	?

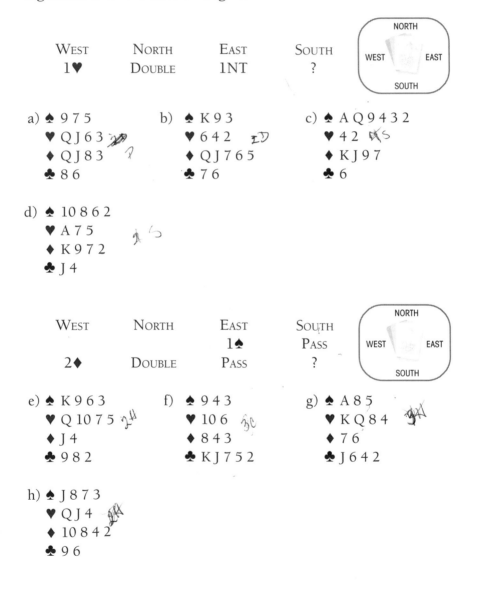

a) ♠ 9 7 5
♥ Q J 6 3
♦ Q J 8 3
♣ 8 6

b) ♠ K 9 3
♥ 6 4 2
♦ Q J 7 6 5
♣ 7 6

c) ♠ A Q 9 4 3 2
♥ 4 2
♦ K J 9 7
♣ 6

d) ♠ 10 8 6 2
♥ A 7 5
♦ K 9 7 2
♣ J 4

WEST	NORTH	EAST	SOUTH
		1♠	PASS
2♦	DOUBLE	PASS	?

e) ♠ K 9 6 3
♥ Q 10 7 5
♦ J 4
♣ 9 8 2

f) ♠ 9 4 3
♥ 10 6
♦ 8 4 3
♣ K J 7 5 2

g) ♠ A 8 5
♥ K Q 8 4
♦ 7 6
♣ J 6 4 2

h) ♠ J 8 7 3
♥ Q J 4
♦ 10 8 4 2
♣ 9 6

Answers to Quiz – Part II

a) **Pass**. East's bid has relieved you from the obligation of bidding. Although you have 6 high-card points, this doesn't look to be the appropriate hand to be competing at the two level.

b) **2♦**. Again you only have six high-card points but, with a decent five-card suit and a useful-looking card in spades, you want to compete for the contract. The hand could belong to your side rather than the opponents . . . or you might push them higher than they would like to be.

c) **4♠**. With 10 high-card points and a six-card spade suit, you want to be in game opposite partner's takeout double. Don't let East's notrump response throw you off. This is the same bid you would make if East had passed.

d) **2♠**. With 8 high-card points you should compete for the contract opposite partner's opening bid strength. With a choice of four-card suits, prefer the major to the minor. Don't be concerned about the location of the high cards.

e) **2♥**. Partner is making a takeout double showing support for the unbid suits, hearts and clubs. Bid the one you prefer.

f) **3♣**. You'll have to go to the three level to bid clubs. Partner presumably has enough strength to be willing to compete to at least that level.

g) **3♥**. With 10 high-card points and a good fit with the suits shown by partner's takeout double, make an invitational bid by jumping a level. Partner can still pass with a minimum, but you want to suggest a game contract if partner has anything extra.

h) **2♥**. This is a situation in which you'll have to bid a three-card suit. Partner asked you to choose between hearts and clubs and this is the best you can do. You can't afford to pass and leave the opponents in 2♦ doubled, and you don't have enough strength to suggest a notrump contract.

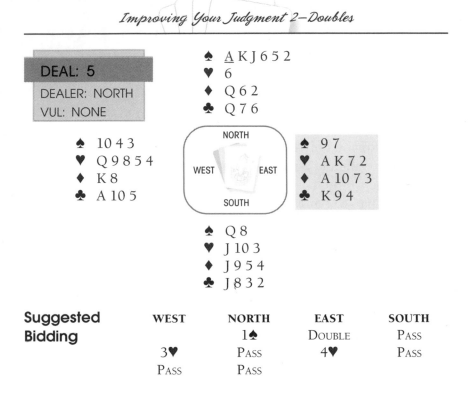

DEAL: 5
DEALER: NORTH
VUL: NONE

♠ A K J 6 5 2
♥ 6
♦ Q 6 2
♣ Q 7 6

♠ 10 4 3
♥ Q 9 8 5 4
♦ K 8
♣ A 10 5

♠ 9 7
♥ A K 7 2
♦ A 10 7 3
♣ K 9 4

♠ Q 8
♥ J 10 3
♦ J 9 5 4
♣ J 8 3 2

Suggested Bidding

WEST	NORTH	EAST	SOUTH
	1♠	DOUBLE	PASS
3♥	PASS	4♥	PASS
PASS	PASS		

North opens the bidding 1♠. East has the right hand for a takeout double with support for the unbid suits and 14 high-card points plus 1 dummy point for the doubleton spade. South, the responder, passes with only 5 high-card points. West, the advancer, has 9 high-card points plus a five-card heart suit. That's enough to make an invitational response by jumping to 3♥, showing about 9–11 points. North doesn't have enough to bid at the three level. East has enough to accept the invitation by bidding 4♥.

If West were to bid only 2♥ in response to the takeout double and North passes, East should pass because West could have no points at all. East-West would then miss their game.

Suggested Opening Lead

North is on lead against 4♥ and would start with the ♠A, top of the touching high cards.

Suggested Play

Declarer has three spade losers, no heart losers unless they are divided 4-0, and a club loser. That's one too many. West can plan to ruff the spade loser in dummy after drawing trumps.

North, however, might start by taking two high spades. On seeing South's doubleton ♠Q[8], North could lead a third round of spades, the ♠J. If declarer ruffs with a low heart, South will overruff and declarer will still have a club loser. If declarer ruffs with the ♥A or ♥K, South will discard. Now declarer will have to lose a trump trick when the missing hearts divide 3-1, and there is still a club loser.

To make the hand, West should not ruff the third round of spades with either a high trump or a low trump in the East hand. Instead, declarer should discard a club from the dummy! The clubs will now be unevenly divided with three in declarer's hand and two in the dummy. The third round of clubs can eventually be trumped. Declarer started with a club loser. By discarding the club, declarer exchanges the club loser for a third spade loser. This is referred to as discarding a *loser on a loser*.

Now the defense is helpless. If North leads another spade, declarer can discard a diamond from dummy and it doesn't matter whether or not South ruffs because West can overruff and draw the remaining trumps. If North leads anything else, declarer wins, draws trumps in three rounds, and then ruffs the club loser with dummy's fourth trump.

Instead of ruffing a spade in dummy . . . and getting overruffed . . . declarer ruffs a club in dummy, after drawing trumps.

Suggested Defense

The best defense is for North to lead three rounds of spades. If declarer doesn't discard a club from dummy, the defenders will get a trump trick, and can later get a club trick as well—in addition to two spade tricks.

---

[8] Technically, South should not play the ♠Q on North's ♠A. The ♠Q conventionally shows either the singleton ♠Q or both the ♠Q and ♠J.

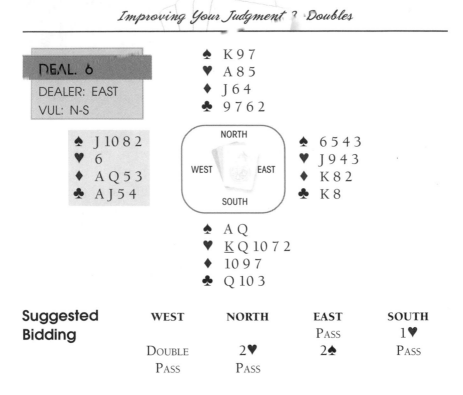

DEAL. 6

DEALER: EAST
VUL: N-S

NORTH
♠ K 9 7
♥ A 8 5
♦ J 6 4
♣ 9 7 6 2

WEST
♠ J 10 8 2
♥ 6
♦ A Q 5 3
♣ A J 5 4

EAST
♠ 6 5 4 3
♥ J 9 4 3
♦ K 8 2
♣ K 8

SOUTH
♠ A Q
♥ K Q 10 7 2
♦ 10 9 7
♣ Q 10 3

Suggested	WEST	NORTH	EAST	SOUTH
Bidding			PASS	1♥
	DOUBLE	2♥	2♠	PASS
	PASS	PASS		

After South opens the bidding 1♥, West makes a takeout double. North raises to 2♥.

East has 7 high-card points and a four-card spade suit. West has asked East to come into the auction and the partnership should have at least half the overall strength and an eight-card spade fit. The quality of the spade suit should not deter East from competing with 2♠. There are two good reasons for bidding. East-West might make a partscore, and the 2♠ bid could push the opponents too high.

East's 2♠ shows about 6–8 points and should end the auction.

Suggested Opening Lead

Against East's 2♠ contract, South would start with the ♥K, top of the broken sequence in the suit bid and raised by the partnership. When the ♥K wins the first trick and South sees the singleton heart in the West hand, South will probably switch to the ♦10, hoping North has something in that suit.

Suggested Play

East's 2♠ contract doesn't look secure because the opponents hold the top three trump tricks. Declarer has at least three spade losers and four heart losers. That's two more than declarer can afford. Declarer has two ways of getting rid of the heart losers: either trumping them in the West hand or discarding them if extra minor suit winners can be established in the dummy.

East should be able to take eight tricks. For example, suppose South wins the ♥K and switches to the ♦10. Declarer can win in the East hand with the ♦K and lead a heart and ruff it in dummy. Declarer can come back to the ♣K, and lead another heart, ruffing in dummy. Declarer can then play the ♣A and ruff a club. Next, declarer can take two more diamond winners. That's eight tricks without drawing trumps.

Another choice would be for East to win South's ♦10 in either hand and lead a trump! The missing trumps are very likely to be divided 3-2, so there's no real danger in drawing a round of trumps. If South wins the ♠Q and leads another diamond, declarer can win and lead a second round of trump. South can win the ♠A, but there's nothing much that the defenders can do at this point. Whatever South leads, declarer can win and start taking winners and ruffing losers, leaving North to take the ♠K at some point as the last trick for the defenders. Declarer doesn't even need to take the club finesse . . . although that works as well. All declarer loses are three trump tricks and a heart trick . . . making an overtrick!

Suggested Defense

There's nothing the defenders can do to prevent declarer from making the 2♠ contract. If the defenders lead trumps to try to prevent declarer from ruffing hearts in dummy, declarer will be able to take winners in diamonds and clubs. If the defenders don't lead trumps, declarer will be able to ruff at least two hearts in dummy and will still have enough winners to make the contract.

If North-South are left to play in 2♥, they may make that contract if West leads the ♠J.

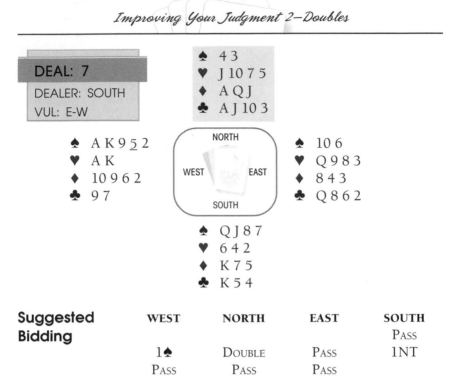

	DEAL: 7		♠ 4 3
	DEALER: SOUTH		♥ J 10 7 5
	VUL: E-W		♦ A Q J
			♣ A J 10 3

♠ A K 9 5 2
♥ A K
♦ 10 9 6 2
♣ 9 7

♠ 10 6
♥ Q 9 8 3
♦ 8 4 3
♣ Q 8 6 2

♠ Q J 8 7
♥ 6 4 2
♦ K 7 5
♣ K 5 4

Suggested	WEST	NORTH	EAST	SOUTH
Bidding				PASS
	1♠	DOUBLE	PASS	1NT
	PASS	PASS	PASS	

South passes. After West opens the bidding 1♠, North has a good hand for a takeout double . . . support for the unbid suits and 13 high-card points plus 1 dummy point for the doubleton spade. East doesn't have anything to say and passes.

South must now decide on the best call. South doesn't have a four-card or longer suit to bid and South's spades aren't long enough or strong enough to pass. West can probably take seven tricks if left to play in 1♠ doubled. With 9 high-card points and some strength in West's suit, South's best choice is 1NT. Even opposite spade shortness in the North hand, South has enough strength to expect to have a reasonable chance of making 1NT.

South's 1NT bid should end the auction. None of the other players has enough to warrant bidding again.

Suggested Opening Lead

Against 1NT, West starts with the ♠5, fourth highest from longest and strongest. Although West holds the ♠A and ♠K, West doesn't have a solid sequence, a broken sequence or an *interior sequence*.

Suggested Play

On the first spade trick, East plays the ♠10 and declarer, South, wins the ♠Q[9]. That gives declarer one spade trick, three diamond tricks, and two club tricks. One more trick is needed.

An extra trick can be developed in the club suit, but South must be aware that East is the *dangerous opponent*. It may seem natural to play the ♣K and then finesse dummy's ♣J or ♣10, hoping West holds the ♣Q . . . especially since West opened the bidding. On this hand, however, if East gains the lead with the ♣Q, East can lead a spade, trapping South's remaining spade honor. East-West will take four spade tricks to go with the ♣Q and their heart winners.

A better choice is to cross to North with a diamond and lead the ♣J, or ♣10, taking a finesse against East. Declarer could play the ♣A first. On the actual hand, the finesse works and South has a seventh trick. Even if the finesse were to lose, declarer would still have a good chance of making the contract. West can't lead spades without giving declarer a second trick in the suit.

Finessing the club into West isn't 100% safe. West might have been able to get to the East hand with a heart so that East can lead a spade. However, West may not realize that this is necessary . . . especially if declarer made the deceptive play of winning the first trick with the ♠Q to make West think that East could hold the ♠J. Or, West may not be able to get to the East hand . . . as on the actual layout of the heart suit.

Suggested Defense

Assuming West starts with a low spade to East's ♠10, the best hope for the defense is that declarer takes the club finesse into the East hand. On winning the ♣Q, East returns the ♠6, partner's suit. West can then take four spade tricks and the ♥A-K. Together with the ♣Q, the defenders win the race to seven tricks.

[9] Winning the ♠Q is more deceptive than winning the ♠J because it leaves West in doubt about who holds the ♠J.

	♠ K 8 5
DEAL: 8	♥ A Q 9 7
DEALER: WEST	♦ 7 4
VUL: BOTH	♣ K J 9 3

	NORTH	
♠ Q 10 7 4		♠ 9 2
♥ 6 2	WEST · EAST	♥ 5 4 3
♦ A K Q J 5		♦ 10 9 2
♣ 7 4	SOUTH	♣ Q 10 8 6 5

♠ A J 6 3
♥ K J 10 8
♦ 8 6 3
♣ A 2

Suggested	**WEST**	**NORTH**	**EAST**	**SOUTH**
Bidding	1♦	DOUBLE	PASS	2♦
	PASS[10]	2♥	PASS	4♥
	PASS	PASS	PASS	

West opens 1♦ and North has the right hand for a takeout double . . . 13 high-card points, 1 dummy point for the doubleton diamond, and support for the unbid suits.

East passes and South knows the partnership belongs in game. South holds an opening bid opposite partner's opening bid. The only question is whether the partnership belongs in 4♥, 4♠ . . . or perhaps even 3NT if North has some strength in diamonds and doesn't have four cards in either major. South could guess to jump to 4♥ or 4♠ . . . but on this hand only a jump to 4♥ would work well. In 4♠, North-South have to lose two diamonds and two spade tricks.

Instead of guessing, South can get additional information from North by cuebidding 2♦. This is forcing, asking North to bid a suit. With only three spades and four hearts, North will choose to bid 2♥. South now has all the information that is necessary to put the partnership in a game contract of 4♥, the known eight-card fit.

---

[10] West might double the 2♦ cuebid to emphasize the diamond suit.

Suggested Opening Lead

Against North's 4♥ contract, East leads the ♦10, top of the touching honors in partner's suit.

Suggested Play

Declarer has a spade loser, two diamond losers, and two club losers. Two losers have to be eliminated. One consideration might be to try both the spade finesse and the club finesse, hoping the missing queens are well placed. On the actual hand, both finesses lose and the contract will go down.

A much safer line of play is to plan to ruff both the club losers in dummy. Then there's no need to rely on any finesses. North-South have all the high hearts, so there is no danger of getting overruffed.

Suppose the defenders start by playing three rounds of diamonds. Declarer has all the high hearts and can confidently ruff the third round of diamonds with the ♥7. East won't be able to overruff even if East started with a doubleton diamond. Now North can play a club to dummy's ♣A, a club back to the ♣K, and ruff a club. West can't overruff. North can play a spade to the ♠K and lead another club and ruff it in dummy. Now declarer can draw three rounds of trump and take the ♠A to make ten tricks.[11]

A slight improvement technically would be for declarer to take the ♠A and ♠K early in the hand before ruffing clubs. Declarer doesn't want a defender discarding spades while the clubs are being ruffed and then being able to ruff one of the spade winners. On this hand, it won't make any difference.

Suggested Defense

There's nothing the defenders can do to prevent declarer from making 4♥. Even if they were to start by leading trump . . . an excellent defense on this hand . . . they can't stop declarer from ruffing two clubs in the dummy and coming to ten tricks.

---

[11] Alternatively, declarer could plan to ruff dummy's fourth spade in the North hand after playing the ♠A, ♠K, and giving up a spade trick. South's trumps could then be used to draw trumps. This is called a dummy reversal.

One instinct you must supress is the urge to raise partner's suit when the bidding is competitive. Your double told a clear story, so if you decide to raise, you need a good reason.

—MIKE LAWRENCE, TAKEOUT DOUBLES

3

Doubler's Rebid and the Subsequent Auction

The classic takeout double is descriptive. It shows the values for an opening bid and support for the unbid suits. After the double, the advancer chooses the trump suit and describes the strength of the hand by the level of the bid. If advancer needs more information, an invitational bid or a cuebid can be made.

As the doubler, when advancer bids at the cheapest level, only with extra strength or favorable distribution should you consider bidding again. Advancer could have no points at all!

A takeout double makes the auction competitive. Both sides are now trying to buy the contract. The doubler and the advancer may have to decide whether to bid more or sell out to the opponents. The auction can proceed in many different ways and you'll frequently have to exercise your judgment since the situation may not be covered in the basic guidelines. That's part of what makes the game interesting and exciting.

Let's take a closer look at the takeout double in action.

Doubler's Rebid

To choose a rebid after making a takeout double, start by considering the strength of the hand in one of three general strength categories:

DOUBLER'S STRENGTH CATEGORIES

Minimum .... 13–16 points
Medium .... 17–18 points
Maximum .... 19+ points

The next step is for the doubler to listen to advancer's bid. It will fall into one of three general categories: 0–8; 9–11; 12 or more. The doubler puts the pieces of the puzzle together:

- With a minimum hand, the doubler usually won't take further action unless advancer has shown some strength.
- With a medium hand, doubler wants to act again even if partner made a minimum advance, showing 0-8 points. There could still be enough combined strength for game or to compete for the contract.
- With a maximum hand, doubler wants to get to game unless advancer has a very weak hand. Let's see how this works.

When Advancer Hasn't Promised Any Strength

You are South and the auction begins:

WEST	NORTH	EAST	SOUTH
		1♣	DOUBLE
PASS	1♥	PASS	?

Advancer was forced to bid and didn't jump to show an invitational hand. You expect partner to be in the 0–8 range. Consider your rebid as the doubler on each of these hands:

1) ♠ Q 8 6 5	2) ♠ K Q 8 6	3) ♠ A Q 8 6
♥ K Q 4	♥ K Q 4 2	♥ K Q 4 2
♦ A J 8 2	♦ A J 8 2	♦ A Q 8 2
♣ 9 2	♣ 9	♣ 9

The first hand falls in the minimum category for the original takeout double and on the rebid doubler should pass. Even if advancer has 8 points, there is not enough combined strength for game. If advancer has 0 points, you are already too high. Don't try to correct partner's choice of hearts as the trump suit. When you chose to make the takeout double it was because you had adequate support for hearts.

Doubler's second hand falls in the medium category . . . 15 high-card points plus 3 dummy points for the singleton club. There could still be game so invite partner to bid again by gently raising to 2♥. With 7 or 8 points, advancer can accept the invitation. If advancer has a weak hand, you shouldn't be too high.

The third hand for the doubler is maximum . . . 17 high-card points plus 3 dummy points. That isn't enough to bid game because advancer could have no points. Instead, offer a strong invitation by jumping to 3♥. This isn't forcing. Advancer can still pass with nothing, but with as little as 5 or 6 points, advancer should bid game.

If opener competes, the doubler should still pass with minimum values. Nothing changes. Suppose East bids again:

West	North	East	South
		1♣	Double
Pass	1♥	2♣	?

With minimum values, South should not compete for the contract. It is up to North to compete with about 6–8 points. With the first hand, South passes, having already described the hand with the takeout double. Any further competition is left to advancer. With the second hand, bid 2♥, showing extra strength and competing for the contract. With the third hand, jump to 3♥ as a strong invitation. Nothing changes.

Examples

You are sitting South. What is your call in the following auction?

WEST	NORTH	EAST	SOUTH
		1♥	DOUBLE
PASS	1♠	PASS	?

```
         NORTH
WEST  [  ]  EAST
         SOUTH
```

♠ K 10 7 5
♥ A 4
♦ K Q 9
♣ J 7 5 3

Pass. Advancer hasn't promised any strength by bidding a suit at the cheapest level. If advancer has a very weak hand, you may already be too high. With enough for your side to belong at the game level, advancer would have made a stronger bid than 1♠.

♠ A K J 4
♥ 9 5
♦ A 8 6 2
♣ K J 6

2♠. Your hand is worth 17 points . . . 16 high-card points plus 1 dummy point for the doubleton. Advancer could have as many as 8 points and the partnership might belong in game. In a competitive auction you can sometimes make game on as few as 24 or 25 points. However, advancer may also have nothing, so raise cautiously.

♠ Q J 8 5
♥ 4
♦ A K Q 5
♣ K J 7 3

3♠. With a maximum hand . . . 16 high-card points plus 3 dummy points for the singleton heart . . . make a highly invitational jump to 3♠. Advancer can accept with about 6–8 but can pass with a very weak hand. By bidding only 3♠ you prevent the partnership from getting too high if the advancer has a very weak hand.

When Advancer Shows Some Values

You are South and the auction starts like this:

West	North	East	South
		1♦	Double
2♦	2♠	Pass	?

Responder's raise to 2♦ removed advancer's obligation to bid, so North is showing some values, about 6–8 points, and is merely competing. With a minimum, doubler should pass. With a medium hand, move toward game. With a maximum hand, get to game. Consider doubler's rebid as South:

1) ♠ Q 8 6 5	2) ♠ K J 8 6	3) ♠ A Q 8 6
♥ K Q 4	♥ K Q 4 2	♥ K Q 4 2
♦ 9 2	♦ 9	♦ 9
♣ A J 8 2	♣ A J 8 2	♣ A Q 8 2

With the first hand, pass because the hand has minimum values. With the second hand, move toward a game by raising to 3♠. The hand has medium values. In the third example, there is enough strength to raise directly to game. Bid 4♠.

When Advancer Makes an Invitational Bid

You are South and the auction starts like this:

West	North	East	South
		1♥	Double
Pass	2♠	Pass	?

Advancer's jump to 2♠ shows an invitational hand of about 9–11 points. With a minimum hand, use your judgment: with 13 or 14 points, doubler will usually decline the invitation by passing;

with 15 or 16 points, doubler will usually accept by bidding game. With a medium or maximum hand, doubler bids game. Consider these hands as South:

1) ♠ Q 8 6 5   2) ♠ K Q 8 6   3) ♠ A Q 8 6
   ♥ 9 2   ♥ 9 2   ♥ 9 2
   ♦ K Q 4   ♦ K Q 4   ♦ K Q 4
   ♣ A J 8 2   ♣ A J 8 2   ♣ A Q 8 2

With the first hand, pass because it is a bare minimum. The second hand is at the top of the minimum range. Accept the invitation and bid 4♠, there should be 25 or more combined points. The third hand is in the medium range and South should bid 4♠. It's rare to consider slam after the opponents have opened the bidding, even with a maximum hand.

Examples

You are sitting South. What is your call in the following auction?

WEST	NORTH	EAST	SOUTH
		1♦	DOUBLE
2♦	3♥	PASS	?

♠ K J 8 5   **Pass.** Advancer's jump shows an invitational
♥ Q 9 7 4   hand, about 9-11 points. It isn't forcing. With
♦ J 2   a minimum for the takeout double, decline the
♣ A J 4   invitation and settle for partscore.

♠ K 9 6 4   **4♥.** You have a medium-strength hand . . . 14
♥ A Q 8 4   high-card points plus 3 dummy points for the
♦ 5   singleton. That's more than enough to accept
♣ K Q 7 2   the invitation.

When Advancer Bids Game

You are South and the auction starts like this:

WEST	NORTH	EAST	SOUTH	
		1♠	DOUBLE	
PASS	4♥	PASS	?	

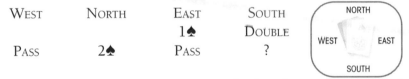

Unless you have a maximum hand and are interested in slam, you should usually pass. Partner has chosen the contract. Partner could have cuebid if interested in getting more information.

When Advancer Makes a Forcing Bid

On some hands, advancer needs more information from doubler and makes a forcing bid. Advancer's only forcing bid is the cuebid of the opponent's suit. You are South and the auction starts like this:

WEST	NORTH	EAST	SOUTH	
		1♠	DOUBLE	
PASS	2♠	PASS	?	

If North cuebids, South must make a further descriptive bid. Bid a five-card suit if you have one. Otherwise, bid your four-card suits up the line,[12] cheapest first, looking for a fit. There's no need to jump with a medium or maximum hand because advancer's cuebid promises another bid and you want to leave room to find your fit. Consider these hands as South:

1) ♠ 5	2) ♠ 5	3) ♠ 8 6
♥ A J 7 3	♥ K Q 7 3	♥ A K 7 3
♦ K J 7 5 4	♦ A 10 8 4	♦ K Q J 4
♣ Q 8 3	♣ Q 9 6 2	♣ A 8 2

---

[12] Four-card suits are generally bid up the line, lower-ranking first, when the auction is likely to continue. They are bid down the line, higher-ranking first, when the auction may not continue.

With the first hand, doubler bids 3♦, with a five-card suit, rather than 3♥. With the second hand, doubler bids 3♣. With a choice among four-card suits, the doubler bids four-card suits up the line. With the third hand, doubler bids 3♦, again bidding four-card suits up the line. There's no need to jump to show the extra values.

Doubler's Cuebid

With a maximum hand for the takeout double, a jump raise of advancer's suit might get the partnership too high. Another way to show a strong hand is to cuebid the opponent's suit after making a takeout double. Suppose the auction starts like this:

WEST	NORTH	EAST	SOUTH
		2♥	DOUBLE
PASS	2♠	PASS	?

NORTH
WEST   EAST
SOUTH

♠ A K 10 8
♥ 7 6
♦ A Q J 5
♣ K Q 5

3♥. The hand is worth 20 points . . . 19 high-card points plus 1 dummy point for the doubleton. A raise to 3♠ would show a medium hand of about 17 or 18 points, but you are stronger than that. Jumping to 4♠, however, would commit the partnership to game and advancer could have no points at all. Cue-bidding the opponent's suit is forcing and shows a very strong hand. If advancer can only rebid 3♠, you can stop in partscore by passing. However, you give advancer the opportunity to bid game with the top of the minimum range.

Doubler's Double

Another way to show a strong hand is to double for a second time if the opponents give you the opportunity. Consider this auction:

WEST	NORTH	EAST	SOUTH
		1♦	DOUBLE
2♦	PASS	3♦	?

♠ A Q 9 6
♥ A K 8 4
♦ 5
♣ A J 8 5

Double. The opponents are making it difficult for you to compete. Advancer didn't make a competitive call over West's raise to 2♦ and is unlikely to have very much. Still, it would be timid not to compete again with this hand. Your second double is still for takeout. Advancer knows you don't have much length or strength in diamonds.

WEST	NORTH	EAST	SOUTH
		1♥	DOUBLE
PASS	2♦	2♥	?

♠ K Q 6 2
♥ J 4
♦ Q 10 5
♣ A K Q 2

Double. Advancer has already chosen a suit but East has competed and won't let you buy the contract so cheaply. You can show the extra strength by doubling for a second time. This denies four-card support for diamonds since you would simply raise to 3♦ to show extra strength. The double asks advancer to pick another suit, rebid diamonds, try notrump, or even pass and defend for penalties with a suitable hand.

Doubler's Rebid with a Strong Overcall

In addition to using the takeout double to show support for the unbid suits, a double is used with a hand too strong for a simple overcall. You are sitting in the South position after the auction has started:

WEST	NORTH	EAST	SOUTH
		1♦	DOUBLE
PASS	1♥	PASS	?

NORTH
WEST EAST
SOUTH

♠ A K J 9 6 5
♥ K 4
♦ A 7 4
♣ J 4

1♠. This hand is too strong for a simple overcall of 1♠. Start with a double. Advancer assumes it is a standard takeout double and chooses a trump suit by bidding 1♥. Now show the true nature of the hand by bidding your suit. Advancer can still pass, but knows you have a hand worth about 18 or more points with a strong preference for spades.

♠ K 7
♥ A K J 10 3
♦ Q 4
♣ K J 9 5

2♥. You doubled intending to subsequently bid hearts, showing a hand too strong for an overcall of 1♥. Advancer surprises you by bidding hearts first. You can now raise to show a medium-strength hand in support of hearts.

Be careful not to bid a new suit when you don't have a strong hand. For example:

♠ A J 6 3
♥ Q 7 4
♦ 6
♣ K Q 8 6 3

Pass. You elected to make a takeout double with this hand rather than overcall the five-card suit . . . a good choice. You hoped advancer would pick spades or clubs, but it hasn't worked out that way. You can't afford to now correct to 2♣ since that would show a hand too strong to overcall 2♣ . . . and you don't have extra strength.

Advancer's Rebid

There's no guarantee you will get another chance to bid after your initial advance over partner's takeout double unless you have cuebid. The auction is competitive, however, so there will be times when you get a second opportunity. This will occur most frequently after you have made a minimum response in the 0–8 point range. There are countless ways the auction might continue after advancer's initial bid. Let's look at some examples. We'll look at both the partnership hands.

NORTH
- ♠ Q 10 6 5 4
- ♥ A 8 6
- ♦ 10 6 4
- ♣ 9 2

	NORTH		
WEST		EAST	
	SOUTH		

SOUTH	WEST	NORTH	EAST	SOUTH
♠ K J 7 3			1♦	DOUBLE
♥ K 9 5 4	PASS	1♠	PASS	2♠
♦ 7	PASS	4♠	PASS	PASS
♣ A K 6 3	PASS			

South makes a takeout double and North bids 1♠. North doesn't have quite enough to make an invitational jump to 2♠. With a medium-strength hand . . . 14 high-card points plus 3 dummy points for the singleton . . . South raises to 2♠ to show the extra strength and interest in game. With a fifth spade and a maximum for the 1♠ bid, North accepts the invitation and bids game.

NORTH
♠ 7 6 4 2
♥ Q 8 2
♦ 10 9 4
♣ 8 5 3

SOUTH	WEST	NORTH	EAST	SOUTH
♠ A K 8 5	1♥	PASS	2♥	DOUBLE
♥ 6	PASS	2♠	PASS	3♥
♦ A Q J 3	PASS	3♠	PASS	PASS
♣ A 10 9 6	PASS			

North makes a minimum advance over South's takeout double but, with a maximum hand, South is still interested in game. A raise to 3♠ would show a hand of about 17–18 points, so South cuebids to show a very strong hand. North has nothing worth mentioning and simply goes back to 3♠. South can't push any further and the partnership settles in partscore. Even 3♠ may be too high.

NORTH
♠ Q J 7 4
♥ 9 8 3
♦ 7 6
♣ Q 6 4 2

SOUTH	WEST	NORTH	EAST	SOUTH
♠ K 5		PASS	1♦	DOUBLE
♥ A K J 10 7 5	PASS	1♠	PASS	2♥
♦ K 8 2	PASS	3♥	PASS	4♥
♣ A 10	PASS	PASS	PASS	

With a hand too strong for a simple overcall, South starts with a takeout double. North assumes this is a standard takeout double and bids the four-card major at the cheapest level. South clarifies that the double is actually based on a strong hand with hearts. With three-card support for hearts and some useful high cards in the other suits, North raises. That's enough to persuade South to try game.

Improving Your Judgment

1. Handling Redoubles

When you double and the opponent on your left (responder) redoubles, your side could be in trouble. The redouble sends the message to opener that the hand belongs to their side. It may be the prelude to a penalty double if you can't find a suitable fit. Consider this hand after the auction begins:

WEST	NORTH	EAST	SOUTH
		1♥	DOUBLE
REDOUBLE	1♠	PASS	?

NORTH

WEST   EAST

SOUTH

♠ K J 8 4
♥ J 6
♦ A Q 8 5
♣ K Q 4

Pass. You have more than a minimum takeout double, but don't consider raising. Partner's bid in this sequence doesn't promise a single point! It merely shows a preference for spades. You have 16 high-card points, East has 13 or more for the opening bid, and West likely has 10 or more for the redouble. That's already 39 points. Not much room for partner to hold anything. 1♠ might already be too high and West might be planning to double for penalty. After the redouble, you are usually simply trying to find a safe resting spot.

2. When Advancer Passes the Takeout Double for Penalty

When advancer passes your low-level takeout double for penalty, lead trumps. Consider this hand after the auction has gone:

WEST	NORTH	EAST	SOUTH
		1♥	DOUBLE
PASS	PASS	PASS	

```
        NORTH
  WEST  [ ]  EAST
        SOUTH
```

♠ Q J 10 4
♥ Q
♦ A K 9 3
♣ K 10 9 3

North has chosen to convert South's double into a penalty double. North must feel that your side has a better chance of taking seven or more tricks with hearts as trumps than their side. Effectively, hearts has become your trump suit. The only way East is likely to make the contract is if you let East score tricks with low trumps. You have a lot of attractive leads, but put the ♥Q on the table. You want to draw trumps and then your side plans to take its winners in the other suits.

3. Revaluing Your Hand

The value of your hand is not constant. It changes as the auction develops. Compare these two hands you might hold as South in the following auction:

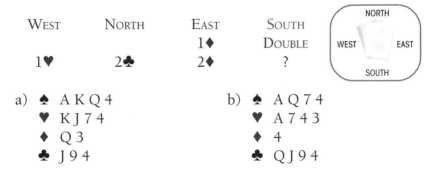

WEST	NORTH	EAST	SOUTH
		1♦	DOUBLE
1♥	2♣	2♦	?

a) ♠ A K Q 4
   ♥ K J 7 4
   ♦ Q 3
   ♣ J 9 4

b) ♠ A Q 7 4
   ♥ A 7 4 3
   ♦ 4
   ♣ Q J 9 4

The first hand includes 16 high-card points and a doubleton diamond but its value has gone down considerably as the auction has progressed. With West bidding hearts, the ♥K and ♥J are likely to be poorly placed. East's diamond rebid indicates that the ♦Q is probably worthless if your side is playing the hand. Partner has chosen to compete in your weakest suit. It looks as if you have too much strength in spades and not enough in clubs. Time to pass.

The second hand has only 13 high-card points but is probably worth a raise to 3♣. You have excellent support for partner; your ♥A is valuable; your singleton diamond will be an asset if you can buy the hand; your ♠A-Q may be worth two tricks if East holds the ♠K. Time to be aggressive and bid 3♣.

4. When Advancer Makes a Responsive Double

If the partnership has agreed to play responsive doubles, then advancer's double of responder's raise is for takeout. Consider these two hands for South after the auction begins:

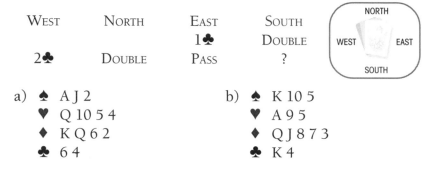

WEST	NORTH	EAST	SOUTH
		1♣	DOUBLE
2♣	DOUBLE	PASS	?

a) ♠ A J 2
   ♥ Q 10 5 4
   ♦ K Q 6 2
   ♣ 6 4

b) ♠ K 10 5
   ♥ A 9 5
   ♦ Q J 8 7 3
   ♣ K 4

With the first hand, bid 2♥. Advancer is likely to have both major suits and is looking for the best fit. With the second hand, bid 2♦. Although advancer is looking for a major suit fit, you don't have four-card support for either major. Diamonds may be the partnership's best trump suit. If not, perhaps you will wind up playing in notrump.

The takeout doubler shows a medium hand by jumping a level. With a maximum hand, the takeout doubler should get the partnership to game.

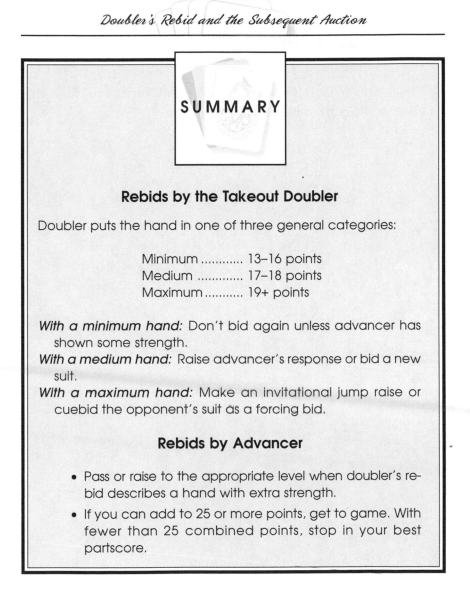

SUMMARY

Rebids by the Takeout Doubler

Doubler puts the hand in one of three general categories:

Minimum .... 13–16 points
Medium .... 17–18 points
Maximum .... 19+ points

With a minimum hand: Don't bid again unless advancer has shown some strength.

With a medium hand: Raise advancer's response or bid a new suit.

With a maximum hand: Make an invitational jump raise or cuebid the opponent's suit as a forcing bid.

Rebids by Advancer

- Pass or raise to the appropriate level when doubler's rebid describes a hand with extra strength.

- If you can add to 25 or more points, get to game. With fewer than 25 combined points, stop in your best partscore.

Quiz – Part I

You are South. What call would you make with each of the following hands after the auction begins:

WEST	NORTH	EAST	SOUTH
		1♥	DOUBLE
PASS	2♣	PASS	?

a) ♠ A Q 6 3
♥ 9 5
♦ K 10 6 2
♣ K J 9

b) ♠ A K 7 4
♥ J 6
♦ Q 9 3
♣ A Q J 6

c) ♠ A J 5 2
♥ 8
♦ A K 8 4
♣ K Q 9 6

d) ♠ A K Q 9 6 2
♥ K 4
♦ K 5
♣ Q 8 4

WEST	NORTH	EAST	SOUTH
		1♠	DOUBLE
1NT	2♦	2♠	?

e) ♠ J 4
♥ A Q 10 3
♦ J 9 7 4
♣ K Q 6

f) ♠ 4 2
♥ A K 8 3
♦ K Q 6 5
♣ A 9 5

g) ♠ 5 4
♥ A K 6 3
♦ Q 9 5
♣ A K J 2

h) ♠ —
♥ K Q 7 4
♦ A Q J 9 3
♣ K 10 4 2

Answers to Quiz – Part I

a) **Pass**. With a minimum hand for the takeout double, don't get the partnership any higher. Partner's advance at the cheapest level hasn't promised any strength.

b) 3♣. With a medium-strength hand, you can raise partner's suit. You may get overboard, but it's worth the risk. Partner could have 7 or 8 points and a game is possible . . . perhaps in notrump.

c) 2♥. With a maximum hand, you want to make a strong invitation to get to game. You could do this by making a jump raise, but that might get you too high and it would take you past the possible game contract of 3NT. Instead, cuebid to show the extra strength. If partner can't do anything more than rebid 3♣, it's time to stop bidding.

d) 2♠. You doubled because you were too strong for a 1♠ overcall. Now finish the description of your hand.

e) **Pass**. Partner has only shown about 6–8 points by bidding 2♦ over responder's bid. With a minimum takeout double, leave any further competition to partner.

f) 3♦. With a medium strength hand, raise partner to the three level. Even if you can't make game, try to get to play the contract in your side's trump fit.

g) **Double**. You have enough to bid again but raising with only three-card support isn't a great idea since partner may have only a four-card suit. Instead, double to show the extra strength. This is still for takeout and partner will know that you don't have four-card support for diamonds.

h) 3♠/5♦. You have an excellent fit with partner and a maximum hand . . . 15 high-card points plus 5 dummy points for the void. You could simply jump to game but slam might even be possible if partner has exactly the right cards. The cuebid is forcing.

Quiz – Part II

You are South. What call would you make with each of the following hands after the auction begins:

WEST	NORTH	EAST	SOUTH	
		1♥	DOUBLE	NORTH
PASS	2♠	PASS	?	WEST EAST
				SOUTH

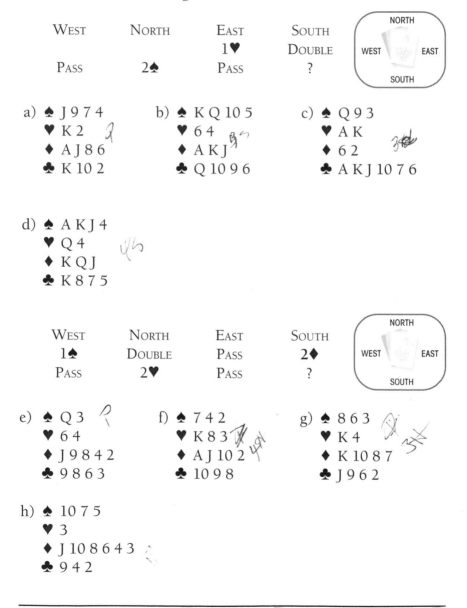

a) ♠ J 9 7 4
   ♥ K 2
   ♦ A J 8 6
   ♣ K 10 2

b) ♠ K Q 10 5
   ♥ 6 4
   ♦ A K J
   ♣ Q 10 9 6

c) ♠ Q 9 3
   ♥ A K
   ♦ 6 2
   ♣ A K J 10 7 6

d) ♠ A K J 4
   ♥ Q 4
   ♦ K Q J
   ♣ K 8 7 5

WEST	NORTH	EAST	SOUTH	
1♠	DOUBLE	PASS	2♦	NORTH
PASS	2♥	PASS	?	WEST EAST
				SOUTH

e) ♠ Q 3
   ♥ 6 4
   ♦ J 9 8 4 2
   ♣ 9 8 6 3

f) ♠ 7 4 2
   ♥ K 8 3
   ♦ A J 10 2
   ♣ 10 9 8

g) ♠ 8 6 3
   ♥ K 4
   ♦ K 10 8 7
   ♣ J 9 6 2

h) ♠ 10 7 5
   ♥ 3
   ♦ J 10 8 6 4 3
   ♣ 9 4 2

Answers to Quiz – Part II

a) **Pass**. Partner's jump is invitational, showing about 9-11 points. With nothing extra for your takeout double, settle for partscore.

b) **4♠**. Accept partner's invitation and bid game.

c) **3♣**. You were intending to bid clubs after doubling to show a hand too strong to overcall 2♣. Partner's invitational bid should not prevent you from describing your hand. Partner may have only a four-card spade suit. 3♣ is forcing, since you are showing extra strength and partner has already made an invitational bid.

d) **4♠**. Even though you have 19 high-card points, slam is unlikely since partner has at most 11 points. Settle for game.

e) **Pass**. Partner is showing a hand too strong to make a simple overcall of 2♥. Even so, it's not worth going any higher on this hand.

f) **4♥**. Having bid only 2♦ at your first opportunity, you couldn't have a better hand in support of hearts. Partner should have about 17 or more points, so game should be reasonable.

g) **3♥**. You have too much to pass but an awkward choice of rebid. Partner is likely to have a good six-card suit in this sequence, so treat your doubleton ♥K-4 as adequate support to raise.

h) **Pass**. You don't much like hearts as trump but bidding again is likely to get the partnership into further trouble.

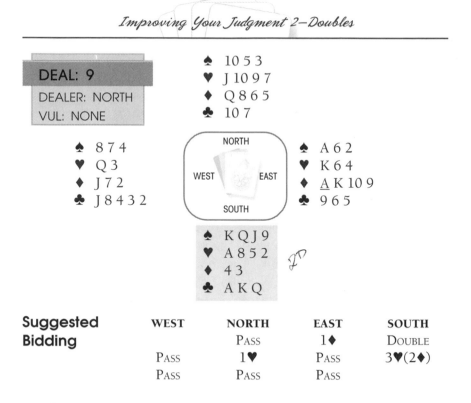

		DEAL: 9			♠ 10 5 3

DEAL: 9
DEALER: NORTH
VUL: NONE

♠ 10 5 3
♥ J 10 9 7
♦ Q 8 6 5
♣ 10 7

WEST
♠ 8 7 4
♥ Q 3
♦ J 7 2
♣ J 8 4 3 2

EAST
♠ A 6 2
♥ K 6 4
♦ A K 10 9
♣ 9 6 5

SOUTH
♠ K Q J 9
♥ A 8 5 2
♦ 4 3
♣ A K Q

Suggested Bidding	**WEST**	**NORTH**	**EAST**	**SOUTH**
		Pass	1♦	Double
	Pass	1♥	Pass	3♥(2♦)
	Pass	Pass	Pass	

North passes. East opens 1♦. South makes a takeout double. After West passes, North has to take the double out and bids 1♥. South, with 19 high-card points plus 1 for the doubleton diamond, has a hand that falls in the maximum category. Although North has bid at the cheapest level, there is still a chance for game if North has the top of the minimum range, so South wants to issue a strong invitation.

There are two ways for South to proceed. A jump to 3♥ shows the maximum and the fit, and invites North to bid game with as few as 5 or 6 points. With only a queen and a jack, North will decline the invitation and settle for partscore.

South's alternative is to cuebid 2♦. With nothing extra to show, North simply rebids 2♥. South can pass this or make one more try by raising to 3♥. That still won't persuade North to go to game.

Suggested Opening Lead

Suppose East is on lead against a 3♥ contract declared by North. East will start with the ♦A, top of the touching high cards.

Suggested Play

Declarer has seven potential losers . . . one spade, two hearts, and four diamonds. Three losers have to be eliminated. North can hope to get rid of two diamond losers, either by ruffing them or by discarding one on the extra club winner and one on the extra spade winner. To make the contract, declarer needs to eliminate a heart loser.

Declarer's best chance is to try a repeated heart finesse. This will work if East holds the ♥K or the ♥Q or both the ♥K and ♥Q. Declarer will lose two trump tricks only if West holds both the ♥K and ♥Q . . . unlikely since East opened the bidding and West didn't bid.

Declarer's challenge is to find two entries to the North hand. East might help by taking the ♦A-K and leading a third round of diamonds. That gives declarer an entry with the ♦Q. However, East might find a stronger defense. After winning the first trick with the ♦A and getting the discouraging signal of the ♦2 from West, East might switch to a club.

After this start, declarer can try to establish an entry to North with the ♠10 by leading the ♠K. If East wins the ♠A and returns a spade or a club, declarer can get to the North hand with the ♠10. Declarer can then lead the ♥J, taking a finesse if East plays low. West wins the ♥Q and may lead a diamond, trapping North's ♦Q. The defenders can then play a third round of diamonds which declarer ruffs in the dummy.

To get back to the North hand to repeat the heart finesse, declarer will have to lead clubs and trump the third high club instead of discarding a loser! Now declarer can lead the ♥10 and trap East's ♥K.

Suggested Defense

East's strongest defense is to switch to a club after winning the ♦A. If declarer leads the ♠K from dummy, East can avoid giving declarer an entry with the ♠10 by refusing to take the ♠A. If declarer leads another high spade from dummy, East can also refuse to win this trick . . . a very imaginative defense. If declarer does lead a third round of spades, East can win the ace and put declarer back in dummy with another club. Declarer can ruff a club winner to get to the North hand once, but that's not good enough to repeat the heart finesse.

If East ducks spades twice, declarer can counter this move by playing three rounds of clubs and discarding the ♠10. Declarer can then play to ruff two diamonds in dummy. The hand offers many challenges for both sides . . . and it's only a partscore!

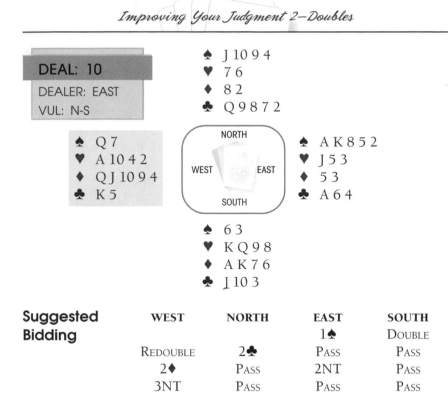

DEAL: 10		♠ J 10 9 4	
DEALER: EAST		♥ 7 6	
VUL: N-S		♦ 8 2	
		♣ Q 9 8 7 2	

♠ Q 7
♥ A 10 4 2
♦ Q J 10 9 4
♣ K 5

NORTH
WEST   EAST
SOUTH

♠ A K 8 5 2
♥ J 5 3
♦ 5 3
♣ A 6 4

♠ 6 3
♥ K Q 9 8
♦ A K 7 6
♣ J 10 3

Suggested Bidding	WEST	NORTH	EAST	SOUTH
			1♠	DOUBLE
	REDOUBLE	2♣	PASS	PASS
	2♦	PASS	2NT	PASS
	3NT	PASS	PASS	PASS

East opens 1♠. South, with 13 high-card points plus 1 dummy point for the doubleton spade, has just enough to make a takeout double.

West, with 12 high-card points and only a doubleton in partner's suit, should start with a redouble. This sends the message to East that the hand should belong to the partnership. It doesn't say much else at this point. West plans to describe the hand on the rebid. West's redouble relieves North of the obligation of bidding. Everyone at the table knows North has very little because East and South have each shown 13 or more points and the redouble shows 10 or more. Nevertheless, with a strong preference for clubs, North should bid 2♣.

East, without quite enough length or strength to double 2♣ for penalty, passes, waiting to see what partner is planning to do. East would be happy to defend if partner wants to double 2♣ for penalty. South should also pass. North has shown a preference for clubs and South has no reason to override that decision.

West doesn't have the right hand to make a penalty double of 2♣. Instead, West bids a new suit, 2♦. After the redouble, this is a forcing bid, showing a five-card or longer suit. North is happy to be out of the auction. East can show the balanced distribution by rebidding 2NT. With 12 high-card points and a five-card suit, West bids 3NT.

If North had not bid 2♣ over the redouble, North-South might get into trouble. South would likely bid 2♦ after East passes. West will double this contract for penalty. Even if North-South now find their way to 3♣, East-West may well decide to double that contract[13].

Suggested Opening Lead

Against a 3NT contract by East, South should lead the ♣J, top of the touching high cards in the suit for which North has shown preference.

Suggested Play

Declarer has to prevent the defenders from promoting and taking too many club tricks before diamond winners can be promoted. To do this, East has to hold up one round of clubs. If South leads a club, declarer might let the defenders win the first trick by playing low from both hands.

Another choice is to win dummy's ♣K and lead a high diamond to drive out South's ♦K. If South leads another club, declarer can duck this trick and win the third round. North will never gain the lead to take the established winners. Declarer can drive out South's ♦A. Declarer gets three spade tricks, a heart, three diamonds, and two clubs. The only play declarer can't make is to win the first trick with the ♣A. Now declarer won't be able to hold up a round of clubs.

Suggested Defense

North-South do best to set up winners in the club suit. This threatens to defeat the contract if North ever gets the lead. Suppose South leads a club and declarer wins dummy's ♣K and leads a diamond. South wins and leads another club. If declarer wins this, the contract can be defeated when South regains the lead. If declarer ducks, South's best play is to lead a low heart. If declarer wins dummy's ♥A, South will again have enough tricks to defeat the contract upon regaining the lead with another diamond winner. However, declarer can counter the heart shift by simply playing low from dummy, instead of playing the ♥A.

[13] Even 2♣ can be defeated two tricks for a penalty of 500 if doubled. However, East-West are unlikely to double 2♣.

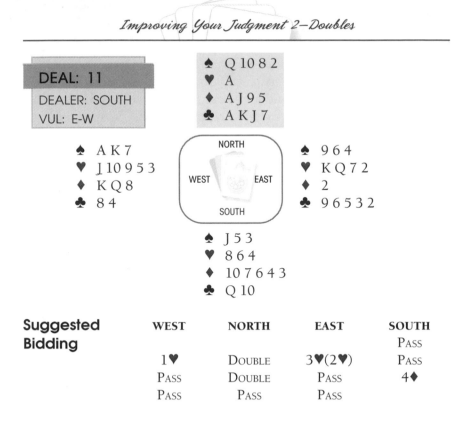

DEAL: 11

DEALER: SOUTH
VUL: E-W

♠ Q 10 8 2
♥ A
♦ A J 9 5
♣ A K J 7

♠ A K 7	♠ 9 6 4
♥ J 10 9 5 3	♥ K Q 7 2
♦ K Q 8	♦ 2
♣ 8 4	♣ 9 6 5 3 2

♠ J 5 3
♥ 8 6 4
♦ 10 7 6 4 3
♣ Q 10

Suggested Bidding

WEST	NORTH	EAST	SOUTH
			PASS
1♥	DOUBLE	3♥(2♥)	PASS
PASS	DOUBLE	PASS	4♦
PASS	PASS	PASS	

South passes. West opens 1♥. North has an excellent hand for a take-out double. East, with four-card heart support and a singleton diamond, should raise to at least 2♥. The modern style is to make a preemptive jump raise to 3♥ with the East hand. This doesn't show a limit raise after the takeout double. It shows a much weaker hand with four-card support. With enough for a limit raise, East would either start with a redouble or use some conventional form of raise over the take-out double, such as *Truscott 2NT*.

South, after East's heart raise, passes with a minimum. West has nothing further to say. North, however, has too much to let the opponents buy the contract in partscore. North can show a strong hand by doubling again. This isn't for penalty; it shows extra strength for the takeout double.

After East passes, South should take out the takeout double into the five-card diamond suit. If East has raised to 3♥, South will have to bid 4♦. South shouldn't be too worried about bidding at the four level.

North has shown a very strong hand by doubling twice and is likely to have four-card support for diamonds. Over 4♠, North might be tempted to gamble on bidding game, but should pass. Having doubled twice and hearing no encouraging bid from South, North has done enough.

Suggested Opening Lead

West is on lead against South's diamond contract and would probably start with the ♥J, the suit bid by the partnership. West might also choose the ♠A, top of the touching honors in that suit.

Suggested Play

Declarer has two spade losers, two heart losers, and two potential diamond losers. That's three too many. The two heart losers can eventually be discarded on dummy's extra club winners, so declarer's main concern is to lose only one diamond trick.

The best way to handle the diamond suit is by taking two finesses, hoping that West started with the ♦K, ♦Q, or ♦K and ♦Q. This will only lose if East started with both the ♦K and ♦Q . . . unlikely on this auction.

After winning a trick with the ♥A, declarer can cross to the South hand by leading dummy's ♣7 to the ♣10. Then declarer can lead a diamond. If West plays low, declarer can finesse dummy's ♦J or ♦9. On the actual hand, this wins immediately and declarer loses only one diamond trick and two spades. If West plays the ♦K or ♦Q when South leads a low diamond, declarer can win with dummy's ♦A and lead a high diamond to force out West's remaining honor.

If the first diamond finesse were to lose to the ♦K or ♦Q in the East hand, declarer would plan to get back to the South hand with the ♣Q and take a second diamond finesse. On the actual layout, this is unnecessary.

Suggested Defense

Provided declarer plays the diamond suit for one loser, the defenders only get three tricks.

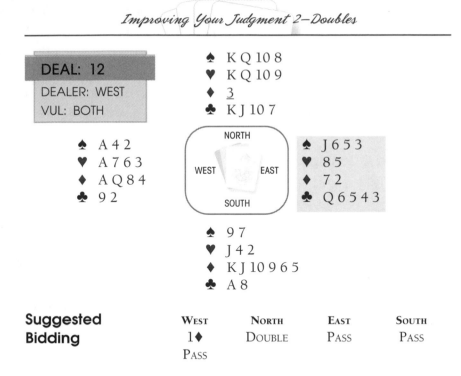

DEAL: 12

DEALER: WEST
VUL: BOTH

♠ K Q 10 8
♥ K Q 10 9
♦ 3
♣ K J 10 7

♠ A 4 2
♥ A 7 6 3
♦ A Q 8 4
♣ 9 2

NORTH

WEST   EAST

SOUTH

♠ J 6 5 3
♥ 8 5
♦ 7 2
♣ Q 6 5 4 3

♠ 9 7
♥ J 4 2
♦ K J 10 9 6 5
♣ A 8

Suggested Bidding

West	North	East	South
1♦	Double	Pass	Pass
Pass			

West has a sound opening bid of 1♦. North, with 14 high-card points and a singleton in the opponent's suit, doubles. After East passes, South must decide what to do. Although North's double is for takeout, South can pass and convert it into a penalty double. It looks as though diamonds may be North-South's best trump suit. South should be able to take three or four tricks in the trump suit along with the ♣A. North should provide some tricks for the takeout double.

West will be aware that the partnership is in trouble when South passes the double, but can't be sure there is a better spot. If West does try to improve the contract, North-South are likely to double whatever contract is reached.

Suggested Opening Lead

Against 1♦ doubled, North leads the ♦3. Although any of the other suits looks attractive, the objective is to draw East-West's trumps as quickly as possible. The high cards in the other suits can wait until later.

Suggested Play

If North leads a trump, declarer, West, will have difficulty taking more than four tricks . . . the ♦A-Q and the ♠A and ♥A. If North doesn't lead a trump, declarer may get at least one more trick.

Suppose North leads the ♥K, instead of a trump. West should let North win this trick. Even if North now switches to a diamond, declarer wins the trick, plays the ♥A and a third heart ruffing in dummy. If North continues with a second heart, Declarer may do even better. Declarer wins the ♥A and ruffs one of the heart losers with dummy's ♦2. Declarer comes back to the West hand with the ♠A and leads a fourth round of hearts, ruffing with the ♦7. South can overruff with the ♦9, but now declarer's ♦8 may eventually become a winner. If declarer can take six tricks, it will be a small triumph.

Suggested Defense

Against a low-level doubled contract, it is usually best to lead trumps. If North leads the ♦3, the defenders can hold declarer to four tricks. South's ♦K is taken by declarer's ♦A and declarer may play two rounds of hearts, trying to ruff a heart in dummy. South should be careful to overtake North's ♥9 or ♥10 with the ♥J to lead the ♦J. That prevents declarer from ruffing a heart loser and also drives out declarer's ♦Q.

On regaining the lead . . . with the ♣A, for example . . . South can draw declarer's remaining two trumps. Declarer only gets the ♦A-Q and two major suit aces . . . down three. That is an excellent result, since North-South may be unable to make nine tricks in notrump if East-West give nothing away.

Some players are so elated when their opponents have stopped bidding in a partscore—instead of bidding a game or a slam—that they always pass; they are afraid if they reopen the bidding the opponents will change their minds and bid game. But you should compete readily in these auctions . . .

— BILL ROOT, COMMONSENSE BIDDING

Balancing
and Other Doubles

When the opponents open the bidding and reach a partscore contract, it's tempting to feel the auction is over. In fact, it might be a relief that the opponents have not bid game. This isn't the time to sit back, however. Your partnership might have as much strength as the opponents and you could also have a suitable trump fit. The double is one of the tools to get back into the auction.

There are advantages and disadvantages to competing. On the positive side, you could make a partscore or even a game. You'll never find out if you aren't in the auction. If the opponents have found an eight-card trump fit, it is very likely that your side also has an eight-card or longer fit in some other suit. If the opponents have a nine-card or longer fit, your side must have at least one eight-card fit in another suit. Why let the opponents choose the trump suit? Also, by competing for the contract, you could push the opponents beyond their comfort level if they still want to come back into the auction.

There are disadvantages to competing. You might be doubled for penalty; you might push the opponents into an excellent contract they would never reach on their own; you might give away information about your distribution or the location of your side's high cards.

In general, there is more to be said in favor of bidding than passing. The takeout double is a powerful tool for competing, even when you are only trying for partscore. Let's take a closer look.

The Balancing Double

Compare these two auctions. In both cases, South is making a takeout double:

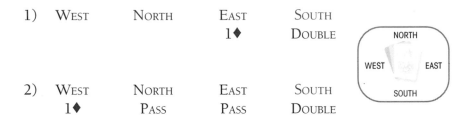

1)	WEST	NORTH	EAST	SOUTH
			1♦	DOUBLE

2)	WEST	NORTH	EAST	SOUTH
	1♦	PASS	PASS	DOUBLE

In the first auction, South is making a takeout double in the *direct position*, directly after an opponent has bid. This is the classic takeout double and South is promising at least the strength for an opening bid and support for the unbid suits. With a hand that is unsuitable for a takeout double, South can pass and wait to see what happens. The auction isn't over and partner still has a chance to act.

In the second auction, South is making a takeout double in the *passout*, or *balancing position*. This is sometimes referred to as a *balancing double*. If South were to pass, the auction is over; the partnership doesn't get another chance to compete for the contract. South, therefore, has to protect the partnership's interest. It's common practice to lower the strength requirements for a takeout double in the balancing position:

DOUBLE IN BALANCING POSITION

- A takeout double in the balancing position can be made with less strength than in the direct position.

This is similar to opening the bidding light in third or fourth position, when partner has already passed. You usually have a full opening bid, but could occasionally open with as few as 10 or 11 points. Likewise, you could have a full takeout double in the balancing position but may have less than in the direct position.

Let's look at the requirements for a balancing double in more detail.

Requirements for a Balancing Double

The commonly used guideline in the balancing position is that you can act with about a king lighter than normal. In other words, 3 fewer points. A direct takeout double shows 13 or more points; a balancing takeout double could be on as few as 10 points, including dummy points. It's as though you take a king out of partner's hand and put it into your hand. Of course, partner has to compensate by removing a king when considering how much to bid . . . more on that shortly.

Although a balancing double can be made with as few as 10 points, it can also be made with 13 or more points as in the direct position.

When the opponents stop at a low level, there is an inference that they have only half the points in the deck. If they hold 26 or more, they would likely bid to game. If they hold close to 26 points, they would at least try for game. So, they probably have about 18-22 points. Since there are 40 high-card points in the deck plus a few extra points for distribution, your side should also hold about 20 points. The strength is likely evenly balanced between the two sides.

Examples

You are sitting South. What is your call in the following auction?

WEST	NORTH	EAST	SOUTH
1♦	PASS	PASS	?

```
        NORTH
  WEST        EAST
        SOUTH
```

♠ Q 8 5
♥ Q 7 4 3
♦ 6 5
♣ A J 7 2

Double. You wouldn't have made a takeout double if East had opened 1♦, but you should take some action in the balancing position. If you pass, the auction is over. A light takeout double will keep the auction going. Partner should have some strength and you might make partscore or push the opponents higher.

♠ K Q 7 2
♥ A Q 6 5
♦ 7
♣ K 10 6 2

Double. This hand is ideal for a takeout double of diamonds in any position. You can have full values to double in the passout chair. Partner will give you a little extra leeway in case you are light, but you can bid again to show a good hand.

♠ Q
♥ K J 2
♦ Q 7 5 3 2
♣ J 9 7 5

Pass. This hand is unsuitable for a takeout double of 1♦. You don't mind defending with diamonds as the trump suit. If you make a balancing bid, you might push the opponents into a better contract.

♠ K 7 4 2
♥ Q 8 6 3
♦ 3
♣ Q 10 5 2

Double. Only 7 high-card points but you do have the ideal shape for a takeout double and can count 3 dummy points for the singleton diamond. This is about as light as you can get. The hand with the shape should stretch to act for the partnership. North might have quite a strong hand that is unsuitable to act over 1♦.

Balancing When You Passed at the First Opportunity

The following hand illustrates the versatility of the take-out double in balancing position:

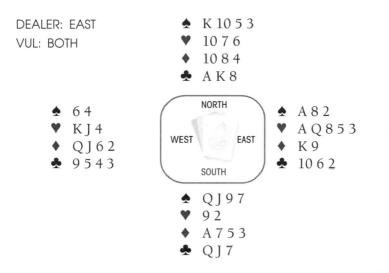

DEALER: EAST
VUL: BOTH

North
♠ K 10 5 3
♥ 10 7 6
♦ 10 8 4
♣ A K 8

West
♠ 6 4
♥ K J 4
♦ Q J 6 2
♣ 9 5 4 3

East
♠ A 8 2
♥ A Q 8 5 3
♦ K 9
♣ 10 6 2

South
♠ Q J 9 7
♥ 9 2
♦ A 7 5 3
♣ Q J 7

Suppose the auction proceeds:

WEST	NORTH	EAST	SOUTH
		1♥	PASS
2♥	PASS	PASS	?

Both sides have 20 combined high-card points: East and West have the high-card points divided 13 + 7; North and South have the strength divided 10 + 10. Each side has an eight-card major suit fit: East-West in hearts; North-South in spades. The side with the higher-ranking suit should win the auction. North-South should be able to compete to 2♠, winning the auction or forcing East-West to bid 3♥ to buy the contract . . . which would be too high.

South is in the balancing position. If South passes, the auction is over. South is looking at 10 points, and there is a strong inference that North also holds about 10 points. East didn't make a move toward game and is likely to have a minimum opening bid. West has only enough to raise to the two level. East has about 13 points and West has about 7 points. With a hand suitable for competing in one of the unbid suits, South can make a light takeout double. In this situation the double shows about 8-12 points, because South would make a takeout double directly with 13 or more points.

Examples

You are sitting South. What is your call in the following auction?

WEST	NORTH	EAST	SOUTH
		1♣	PASS
2♣	PASS	PASS	?

♠ K 10 9 7
♥ Q J 5 3
♦ K 8 5
♣ 8 2

Double. If you don't do something, the auction will be over. It sounds as though the opponents have only half the points in the deck. Partner likely has about 10 points. Take a chance and get into the auction.

♠ A 3
♥ K 9 6 2
♦ J 7 6 5
♣ Q J 8

Pass. A stronger hand than the previous example, but it is unsuitable for a balancing takeout double. If partner were to choose spades, you could be on a 4-2 fit at the two level. You have too much of your strength in clubs to do anything except defend.

Advancing a Balancing Double

When partner makes a double in the balancing position, proceed with caution. Partner could have full values for the takeout double but could also have as few as 10 points. When the opponents stop in a partscore, partner is going to assume you have some strength. Partner could have borrowed a king from your hand to make a balancing bid.

ADVANCING A BALANCING DOUBLE

- Compensate slightly: bid at the cheapest level with 0-10; jump a level with 11-14; bid game or cuebid with 15 or more.

Consider the following auctions. You are South.

WEST	NORTH	EAST	SOUTH
		1♥	PASS
PASS	DOUBLE	PASS	?

♠ A Q 8 2
♥ J 8 7
♦ Q 4 3
♣ J 8 2

1♠. With 10 high-card points you would make an invitational jump to 2♠ if partner made a takeout double in the direct seat. Over partner's double in the balancing position, 1♠ is enough. Partner may have stretched to keep the auction going with as few as 8 or 9 points. If the partnership has enough combined strength for game, partner will take another bid.

♠ 7 4 3
♥ A J 8 3
♦ Q 6 2
♣ K 9 2

1NT. This might be worth a jump to 2NT if partner were not in the balancing position. Partner is already expecting you to have about 10 points in this auction, so don't get the partnership too high.

♠ 5 3
♥ A 8 4 3
♦ K Q
♣ Q J 9 7 6

3♣. This is more than partner could expect. An invitational jump to 3♣ seems about right. That shouldn't be too high even if partner has stretched to make a takeout double. If partner has a good hand, you should be able to get to game.

♠ K Q 4 3
♥ A J 4
♦ K 8
♣ 10 7 4 2

2♥. With an opening bid, you would take the partnership to game opposite a direct takeout double. Opposite a balancing double, that might be too high. One way to show the strength is to start with a cuebid. If partner bids 2♠, you can then make a highly invitational raise to 3♠. If partner bids 2♦, you can invite with 2NT. A cuebid opposite a balancing double is not forcing to game.

West	North	East	South	
1♣	Pass	2♣	Pass	NORTH
Pass	Double	Pass	?	WEST ⬚ EAST
				SOUTH

♠ Q 7 4
♥ A K 6 3
♦ 9 4
♣ K 7 6 2

3♥. If the partnership had enough combined strength for game, partner would likely have made a takeout double at the first opportunity. Partner is making only a balancing double.

Other Doubles

Doubling as a Passed Hand

If you pass originally, when you had an opportunity to open, you become a *passed hand*.[14] That doesn't mean you are out of the auction forever. Consider the following auctions when you are sitting South.

West	North	East	South	
			Pass	NORTH
Pass	Pass	1♣	?	WEST ⬚ EAST
				SOUTH

---

[14] If right hand opponent opens and you pass, you are not technically considered a passed hand because you did not have an opportunity to open the bidding. You could have quite a good hand unsuitable for a takeout double or an overcall.

♠ 4
♥ A J 9 7
♦ Q 10 6 2
♣ K J 8 3

Double. With 11 high-card points, you pass in opening chair. When the bidding comes around a second time, the hand is worth a takeout double. Revalue the hand by adding 3 dummy points for the singleton spade. You could make a partscore or push the opponents to an uncomfortable spot.

WEST	NORTH	EAST	SOUTH	
		PASS	PASS	NORTH
1♦	PASS	1♥	?	WEST EAST
				SOUTH

♠ Q J 9 3
♥ 8 5
♦ 9 6 2
♣ A K 10 2

Double. You have support for the unbid suits and have already passed. Partner isn't going to expect too much. It's a bit dangerous to come in at this point since partner could have nothing, but if you never take any chances . . .

WEST	NORTH	EAST	SOUTH	
			PASS	NORTH
3♥	PASS	PASS	?	WEST EAST
				SOUTH

♠ K J 7 4
♥ 8
♦ Q 10 9 5
♣ A 10 8 2

Double. The auction is uncomfortably high but you should act. Don't let the opponents preempt you out of the auction without a struggle. Partner can have quite a good hand but be unable to bid directly over 3♥. Partner might have a borderline takeout double or overcall but may be cautious because you passed originally.

This last hand illustrates an important principle in competitive auctions: the hand with the shape should take the action. Even if you have to stretch a little, it is your responsibility to protect the partnership's interest by overcalling or doubling with a suitable hand. In the above auction, partner might hold a hand like this and be waiting for you to double:

♠ A 4
♥ A Q 10 7
♦ K 4 3
♣ 9 5 4 3

Partner can't double 3♥ for takeout but will be happy to pass your double and collect a large penalty.

Takeout Doubles by Opener

You can make a takeout double after you have opened the bidding. Suppose you are South in the following auctions:

WEST	NORTH	EAST	SOUTH
			1♥
1♠	PASS	2♠	?

♠ 3
♥ A K 10 8 5
♦ K J 7 5
♣ A K J

Double. With 19 high-card points and a five-card suit, you are unwilling to sell out to the opponents' 2♠ partscore. Having already shown a five-card heart suit, double is more flexible than bidding 3♦ since it leaves partner the option of bidding clubs.

WEST	NORTH	EAST	SOUTH
			1♠
2♦	PASS	PASS	?

♠ K Q 10 7 3
♥ A Q 8 4
♦ 6
♣ K Q 2

Double. With shortness in the opponent's over-called suit, make a takeout double with this type of hand. This is sometimes referred to as a *reopening double* because you are reopening the auction when you could have ended it by passing. Double is more flexible than 2♥ since it leaves open the possibility of playing in clubs and also allows partner to pass for penalties with some length and strength in diamonds.

Takeout Doubles by Responder

Responder can also make a takeout double.[15] Consider this hand as South in the following auction:

WEST	NORTH	EAST	SOUTH
	1♣	1♥	1♠
2♥	PASS	PASS	?

♠ A J 8 4 3
♥ 9
♦ Q 7 4 2
♣ K 8 5

Double. With 10 high-card points you have too much to let the opponents buy the contract in their heart fit at the two level. Double at this point is not for penalty. Having already shown the spades, double is the most flexible bid you can make. It says, "Do something partner!"

Partner can show spade support, bid notrump, rebid clubs, or even try diamonds. Partner can also pass, converting your reopening double into a penalty double.

Improving Your Judgment

The takeout double is a powerful tool that provides scope for judgment. Here are tips to help expand the use of the call.

1. Do Not Disturb

Balancing is generally a good idea. Be careful, however, not to disturb the opponents when they are in a poor contract. If you give them another chance, they may find a better spot. Compare these two hands for South after the auction begins:

WEST	NORTH	EAST	SOUTH
1♥	PASS	PASS	?

---

[15] The negative double is another form of takeout double, used when partner opens the bidding in a suit at the one level and the opponent on your right overcalls. Negative doubles deserve a whole book to themselves.

a)   ♠ K 8 5 3   b)   ♠ 5 3
      ♥ 10 4   ♥ K J 10 8 4
      ♦ Q 9 7 3   ♦ Q 9 7 3
      ♣ K J 4   ♣ K 4

Both hands have only 9 high-card points. With the first hand, make a takeout double. The hand has support for the unbid suits and partner will expect that you might be a little light in the balancing position, protecting the interest of your side. With the second hand, pass. You don't have a suitable hand for a takeout double and are happy to defend with hearts as the trump suit. Partner is unlikely to have a good hand and is probably short in hearts but did not overcall or double. If you take any action with this hand, North-South could find a better contract.

You generally want to make a balancing call when the opponents are comfortably resting in a suitable trump fit. Compare these two auctions when you are South:

a)

WEST	NORTH	EAST	SOUTH
1♦	PASS	1♠	PASS
2♠	PASS	PASS	?

b)

WEST	NORTH	EAST	SOUTH
1♦	PASS	1♠	PASS
1NT	PASS	PASS	?

```
        NORTH
 WEST          EAST
        SOUTH
```

In the first auction, East-West have found a spade fit and have stopped comfortably in partscore. This is usually a good time for South to balance with a suitable hand. In the second auction, the opponents have not found a fit. West didn't raise spades and East didn't support diamonds. Although the opponents have stopped in a partscore, it is more dangerous to balance on a marginal hand. West, for example, could easily hold four hearts or four clubs in this auction.

2. Delaying Action

Sometimes your hand is unsuitable for an immediate takeout double but becomes suitable after the opponents have found a fit. Consider this auction.

WEST	NORTH	EAST	SOUTH	
		1♦	PASS	
1♥	PASS	2♥	DOUBLE	

In this auction South is making a takeout double of hearts. South couldn't make a takeout double of diamonds, presumably because South doesn't have support for hearts but does have some length and strength in diamonds, something like this:

♠ A J 8 3
♥ 8
♦ A Q 7 4
♣ K 10 6 3

3. Be Flexible and Open Minded

Doubles of low level bids are generally for take-out. Here's an example where you might want to make an exception:

SOUTH
♠ Q 9 7 3 2
♥ 6
♦ Q 8 6 2
♣ J 6 4

WEST	NORTH	EAST	SOUTH	
1♥	PASS	1NT	PASS	
2♥	DOUBLE	PASS	?	

In this auction, partner is making a penalty double of 2♥ and you should pass and defend. Partner is not in the balancing position. If partner had passed, you would still have an opportunity to bid. If partner wanted to make a takeout double of hearts, partner would have doubled at the first opportunity. Finally, the opponents have not necessarily found a fit. East did not support hearts and may have a singleton or void. The two hands could be:

NORTH
♠ 6
♥ A Q 10 3 2
♦ A K 6
♣ A 7 5 3

SOUTH
♠ Q 9 7 3 2
♥ 6
♦ Q 8 6 2
♣ J 6 4

4. Balancing Notrump Bids

When you take action in the balancing position, partner is going to assume you have a weaker hand than in direct position. This is true of a takeout double and is also true when you bid notrump. Consider the following auction. You are South:

WEST	NORTH	EAST	SOUTH
1♥	PASS	PASS	1NT

A direct overcall of 1NT shows about 15–18 points. A balancing overcall shows approximately a king less, about 12–14 points. In balancing position, if you have a balanced hand of about 15–17 points, start with a takeout double, planning to rebid notrump at the cheapest available level.

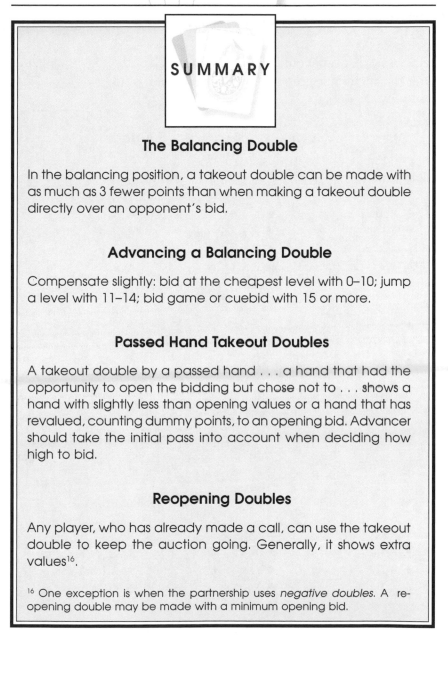

SUMMARY

The Balancing Double

In the balancing position, a takeout double can be made with as much as 3 fewer points than when making a takeout double directly over an opponent's bid.

Advancing a Balancing Double

Compensate slightly: bid at the cheapest level with 0–10; jump a level with 11–14; bid game or cuebid with 15 or more.

Passed Hand Takeout Doubles

A takeout double by a passed hand . . . a hand that had the opportunity to open the bidding but chose not to . . . shows a hand with slightly less than opening values or a hand that has revalued, counting dummy points, to an opening bid. Advancer should take the initial pass into account when deciding how high to bid.

Reopening Doubles

Any player, who has already made a call, can use the takeout double to keep the auction going. Generally, it shows extra values[16].

[16] One exception is when the partnership uses *negative doubles*. A reopening double may be made with a minimum opening bid.

Quiz – Part I

As South, what call would you make with each of the following hands after the auction begins:

WEST	NORTH	EAST	SOUTH
1♦	PASS	PASS	?

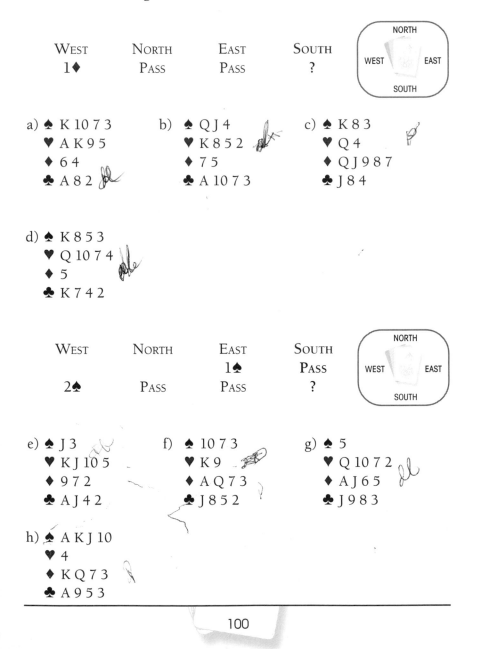

a) ♠ K 10 7 3
   ♥ A K 9 5
   ♦ 6 4
   ♣ A 8 2

b) ♠ Q J 4
   ♥ K 8 5 2
   ♦ 7 5
   ♣ A 10 7 3

c) ♠ K 8 3
   ♥ Q 4
   ♦ Q J 9 8 7
   ♣ J 8 4

d) ♠ K 8 5 3
   ♥ Q 10 7 4
   ♦ 5
   ♣ K 7 4 2

WEST	NORTH	EAST	SOUTH
		1♠	PASS
2♣	PASS	PASS	?

e) ♠ J 3
   ♥ K J 10 5
   ♦ 9 7 2
   ♣ A J 4 2

f) ♠ 10 7 3
   ♥ K 9
   ♦ A Q 7 3
   ♣ J 8 5 2

g) ♠ 5
   ♥ Q 10 7 2
   ♦ A J 6 5
   ♣ J 9 8 3

h) ♠ A K J 10
   ♥ 4
   ♦ K Q 7 3
   ♣ A 9 5 3

Answers to Quiz – Part I

a) **Double**. This is a normal takeout double. It doesn't matter that you are in the passout position except that partner will proceed more cautiously . . . under the assumption that you could have less than opening values. You can show partner that you have a sound takeout double by bidding again.

b) **Double**. You wouldn't double if the 1♦ opening bid had been on your right. In the balancing position, however, you can borrow 3 points. That gives you enough to make a takeout double.

c) **Pass**. You don't have the right type of hand to make a takeout double. You're comfortable defending with diamonds as the trump suit. If you bid, the opponents might reach a better spot.

d) **Double**. This is about as light as it gets but you don't want to give up on the auction without a fight. Partner should have about 10 points since West only opened at the one level and East did not have enough to respond.

e) **Double**. You didn't double directly, so partner isn't going to expect too much. The opponents have found a fit and stopped at a low level, so you are making a balancing double.

f) **Pass**. You have the strength but not the distribution to make a balancing double. If you double, partner might choose hearts and you could land in a 4-2 fit at the three level.

g) **Double**. Go for it. You might consider passing at unfavorable vulnerability . . . if your side is vulnerable and their side is not. Otherwise, you should get your side into the auction.

h) **Pass**. You have enough to double 2♠ for penalty. Unfortunately, double would be for takeout. You'll have to sit back and defend with this hand. At least you're headed for a plus score.

Quiz – Part II

You hold this hand as South. What call would you make in each of the following auctions?

♠ K 7 3 2
♥ 8 4
♦ K 8 2
♣ A 9 7 3

	WEST	NORTH	EAST	SOUTH	
a)			1♦	PASS	NORTH
	PASS	DOUBLE	PASS	? 1♠	WEST EAST
					SOUTH
b)	WEST	NORTH	EAST	SOUTH	
		PASS	1♣	PASS	
	1♥	DOUBLE	2♥	? 2♠	
c)	WEST	NORTH	EAST	SOUTH	
	1♥	PASS	1NT	PASS	
	2♥	DOUBLE	PASS	?	
d)	WEST	NORTH	EAST	SOUTH	
		1♦	PASS	1♠	
	2♥	PASS	PASS	?	
e)	WEST	NORTH	EAST	SOUTH	
				PASS	
	PASS	PASS	1♥	?	

You hold this hand as South. What call would you make in the following auction?

♠ A Q 7
♥ K Q 10
♦ Q 8 4 2
♣ K J 5

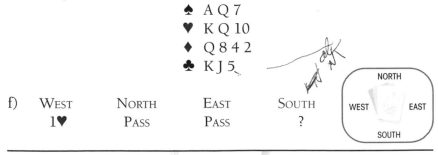

	WEST	NORTH	EAST	SOUTH	
f)	1♥	PASS	PASS	?	NORTH
					WEST EAST
					SOUTH

Answers to Quiz – Part II

a) **1♠**. Partner is making a takeout double in the balancing position and could have less than opening values. No need to jump. If the partnership has enough for game, partner will likely take another call.

b) **2♠**. Partner is making a takeout double for the unbid suits, spades and diamonds. You have enough to compete but not enough to invite partner to game. Remember, partner passed initially.

c) **Pass**. Partner is not in the balancing position and is not making a takeout double. Partner would have doubled 1♥ at the first opportunity with a takeout double. Instead, partner is making a penalty double. East-West haven't found a fit. East may have a singleton or void in hearts.

d) **Double**. As responder, you don't want to let West buy the contract in 2♥ when your partner has enough to open the bidding. A reopening double is the most flexible call you can make. It says you want to take some further action but don't have a clear cut bid. With some length and strength in hearts, partner might want to leave the double in for penalties.

e) **Double**. You passed originally, so partner won't be expecting a full opening bid. You are showing interest in competing in one of the unbid suits.

f) **Double**. With 17 high-card points, you are too strong to bid 1NT in the balancing position, which would show about 12-14 points. Instead, start with a double, planning to rebid notrump at your next opportunity.

DEAL: 13

DEALER: NORTH
VUL: NONE

♠ J 9 7 3
♥ 10 5
♦ J 3
♣ J 9 6 4 3

NORTH

WEST   EAST

SOUTH

♠ Q 4
♥ Q 8 3
♦ 10 8 7 6 5
♣ A K 2

♠ K 8 6 5
♥ 7 2
♦ A K 4 2
♣ 8 7 5

♠ A 10 2
♥ A K J 9 6 4
♦ Q 9
♣ Q 10

Suggested Bidding

WEST	NORTH	EAST	SOUTH
	Pass	Pass	1♥
Pass	Pass	Double	2♥
3♦	Pass	Pass	Pass

South opens 1♥. The West hand is not suitable for a takeout double. It doesn't have enough strength and, more importantly, without support for the unbid suits it doesn't have the right shape. Also, it doesn't have a good enough suit to overcall at the two level. West should pass. North, with only 3 high-card points plus 1 length point, passes.

East is in the balancing position, with the option of bidding or passing and ending the auction. With 10 high-card points plus 1 dummy point for the doubleton heart, East would not have quite enough to make a takeout double directly over an opening bid. In the passout chair, however, East can make a lighter takeout double to balance out the auction. East knows that West must hold some strength because the opponents have stopped at the one level.

South has a good hand and can show the extra strength and good suit by bidding 2♥ over the double, trying to make it more difficult for East-West to find their best contract. West has 11 high-card points and a five-card suit. That would be enough to make an invitational jump response over a standard takeout double. When partner doubles in the balancing position, however, West should be more cautious. In effect, East is already counting on West for about 10 points in this auction. Also, East passed initially, so West should settle for 3♦. West's 3♦ call is likely to end the auction.

Suggested Opening Lead

North is on lead against a 3♦ contract and would start with the ♥10, top of the doubleton in partner's suit.

Suggested Play

Declarer has a spade loser, three heart losers, a diamond loser unless the diamonds are divided 2-2, and a club loser. Declarer can plan on ruffing a heart loser in dummy. Alternatively, the ♥Q might become a winner if South has both the ♥A and ♥K, as seems likely from the auction. However, it may get trumped by North.

For example, South wins the ♥A and ♥K and then leads a third round. West's ♥Q may be ruffed with the ♦J. If declarer overruffs with dummy's ♦K, South's ♦Q will become a winner, even though the missing diamonds were originally divided 2-2.

Declarer can counter this defense by discarding a club loser from dummy instead of overruffing. Declarer had to lose a club trick anyway, so declarer is discarding a loser on a loser. This prevents the loss of a trump trick. When declarer regains the lead, the ♦A-K can be played to draw the opponents' outstanding trumps. Now declarer's club loser can be ruffed in dummy. Declarer doesn't lose a club trick.

Suggested Defense

As discussed above, the best defense is for South to lead three rounds of hearts. North ruffs the third round with the ♦J. If declarer overruffs, the contract is likely to be defeated if the defenders can establish a club winner to go with their spade winner.

If declarer chooses to discard a club from dummy instead of overruffing, North can lead a spade to South's ♠A and South can lead another heart, hoping North has another high diamond. Unfortunately for the defenders, North's remaining diamond is the ♦3. If North held a slightly higher diamond, this defense would succeed in holding declarer to eight tricks . . . nice try!

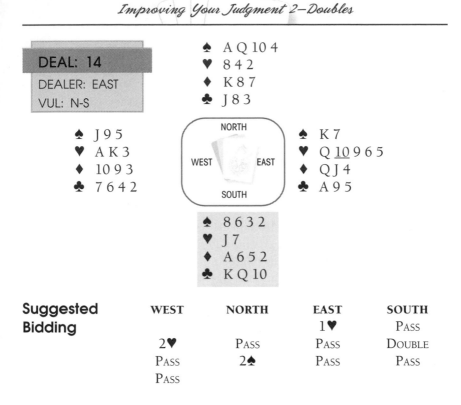

	♠ A Q 10 4		
DEAL: 14	♥ 8 4 2		
DEALER: EAST	♦ K 8 7		
VUL: N-S	♣ J 8 3		

♠ J 9 5		♠ K 7
♥ A K 3	NORTH	♥ Q 10 9 6 5
♦ 10 9 3	WEST · EAST	♦ Q J 4
♣ 7 6 4 2	SOUTH	♣ A 9 5

| ♠ 8 6 3 2 |
| ♥ J 7 |
| ♦ A 6 5 2 |
| ♣ K Q 10 |

Suggested	**WEST**	**NORTH**	**EAST**	**SOUTH**
Bidding			1♥	PASS
	2♥	PASS	PASS	DOUBLE
	PASS	2♠	PASS	PASS
	PASS			

East opens 1♥. South, with only 10 high-card points plus 1 dummy point for the doubleton heart, isn't strong enough for an immediate takeout double. Partner would expect a stronger hand. West has enough to raise East's hearts to the two level. North, with 10 high-card points, doesn't have enough to take any direct action. East, with a minimum opening, passes and the auction returns to South.

After East passes the raise to 2♥, South is in the balancing position. If South passes, East-West buy the contract in hearts. South knows partner has some strength because the opponents have settled for partscore. To compete for the auction, South can make a balancing takeout double. Partner won't be expecting too much strength because South didn't make a takeout double of 1♥.

After West passes, North bids 2♠. Although North has 10 high-card points, there's no need to make an invitational jump. South would have doubled earlier with an opening bid or more. North's 2♠ call should end the auction.

Suggested Opening Lead

Against North's 2♠ contract, East will probably choose the ♥10, top of the touching high cards from an interior sequence in the suit that the partnership has bid and raised.

Suggested Play

The declarer, North, has two potential spade losers assuming the missing spades are divided 3-2, three heart losers, a diamond loser, and a club loser. Two losers have to be eliminated. One of the heart losers can be ruffed in dummy, so declarer can make the contract by restricting the spade losers to one.

Declarer might consider a simple finesse of the ♣Q, hoping West holds the ♣K, but this is unlikely to work. On the opening lead, West wins the ♥K and, likely, takes the ♥A as well. That doesn't leave much for East's opening bid. Also, West might have bid more holding the ♠K in addition to the ♥A-K. So, it's likely that East holds the ♠K.

Instead of finessing the ♣Q, declarer could consider finessing the ♠10, hoping West holds the ♠J[17]. On the actual hand, this works well. If declarer does take a first round finesse of the ♣Q, losing to East's ♠K, declarer can still recover by taking a subsequent finesse against West's ♠J.

Suggested Defense

There is nothing the defenders can do to prevent declarer from taking eight tricks with spades as trump, provided declarer doesn't lose two trump tricks.

If left to play in 2♥, East can take exactly eight tricks. East has one spade loser . . . thanks to the favorable location of the ♠A . . . two diamond losers, and two club losers. The missing hearts divide 3-2, so declarer has no loser in that suit.

---

[17] Since East is known to hold the ♠K, declarer's technically correct line is to play the ♠A first, to guard against a singleton ♠K. This will also prove successful if East holds the doubleton ♠K-J. On the actual layout, East plays the ♠7 on the first round. Declarer can then cross to dummy and lead a spade, finessing the ♠10 when West follows with the ♠9. This forces East's ♠K.

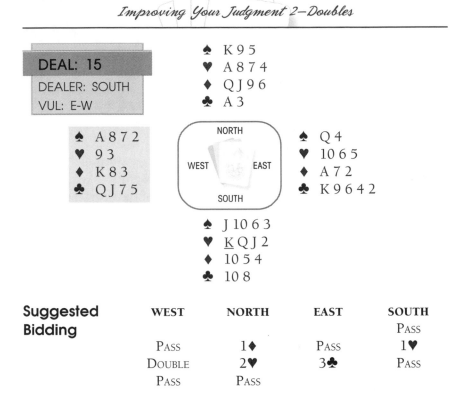

DEAL: 15

DEALER: SOUTH
VUL: E-W

```
              ♠ K 9 5
              ♥ A 8 7 4
              ♦ Q J 9 6
              ♣ A 3
♠ A 8 7 2          NORTH          ♠ Q 4
♥ 9 3                             ♥ 10 6 5
♦ K 8 3      WEST        EAST     ♦ A 7 2
♣ Q J 7 5                         ♣ K 9 6 4 2
                   SOUTH
              ♠ J 10 6 3
              ♥ K Q J 2
              ♦ 10 5 4
              ♣ 10 8
```

Suggested Bidding	WEST	NORTH	EAST	SOUTH
				PASS
	PASS	1♦	PASS	1♥
	DOUBLE	2♥	3♣	PASS
	PASS	PASS		

South and West pass. North opens the bidding 1♦. East, with only 9 high-card points, doesn't have enough to overcall in the weak five-card club suit. South responds 1♥, bidding four-card suits up the line.

At this point, West can make a takeout double, showing support for the unbid suits, clubs and spades. Partner isn't going to expect a full opening bid since West passed originally. West's double shouldn't stop North from raising to 2♥ . . . the same bid North would make if West passed.

With 9 points, East can now compete for the contract by bidding 3♣. East knows the partnership has about half the overall strength and that West's double shows good support for clubs. East's 3♣ call should end the auction as all of the other players have already described their hands.

Suggested Opening Lead

South is on lead against East's 3♣ contract and would start with the ♥K, top of the solid sequence.

Suggested Play

In 3♣, the declarer has a spade loser, three heart losers, a diamond loser, and a club loser. That's two too many. One of the heart losers can be ruffed in dummy but declarer will need to get rid of a diamond loser, or a spade loser, to make the contract.

Declarer's plan should be to try to develop an extra spade winner with the ♠Q. This can be done by leading a low spade from dummy, hoping North holds the ♠K. If North plays low, declarer can win the ♠Q and won't have a spade loser. If North rises with the ♠K, declarer plays low. Declarer later takes the ♠Q, goes to the dummy, and plays the ♠A and throws away a diamond loser.

The defenders may spoil declarer's plan (see below) but suppose North-South take the first two heart tricks and then switch to a diamond. Declarer must win dummy's ♦K and lead a low spade. If North rises with the ♠K and leads another diamond, East wins the ♦A and takes the ♠Q. East can then ruff a heart to get to dummy and discard the diamond loser on dummy's ♠A. Then declarer can start to draw trumps. Declarer loses a spade, two hearts, and a club.

Suggested Defense

The defenders have an opportunity to defeat 3♣ after South leads the ♥K. Instead of encouraging South to continue with another heart winner, North can make a discouraging signal with the ♥4. Although the ♥K wins the first trick, South should recognize partner's ♥4 as a low card. South holds the ♥2 and can see the ♥3. Since North bid diamonds, South might conclude that partner would like a switch to diamonds, instead of continuing hearts. If South switches to diamonds, the defenders can win the race.

Declarer can win dummy's ♦K and lead a spade, but North can win the ♠K and lead a second round of diamonds. Declarer can win the ♦A and take a trick with the ♠Q. Because the defenders haven't taken a second heart trick, declarer doesn't have a quick entry to the dummy to take the ♠A. Whether declarer leads a heart or a club, the defenders can win and take a diamond trick to defeat the contract.

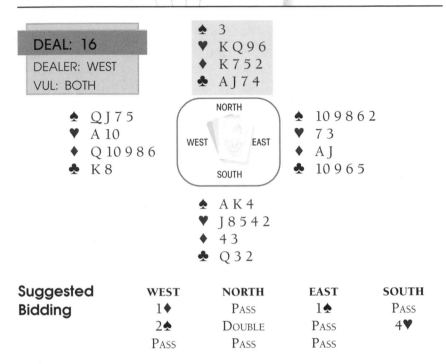

DEAL: 16		NORTH	♠ 3

DEAL: 16
DEALER: WEST
VUL: BOTH

♠ 3
♥ K Q 9 6
♦ K 7 5 2
♣ A J 7 4

♠ Q J 7 5
♥ A 10
♦ Q 10 9 8 6
♣ K 8

♠ 10 9 8 6 2
♥ 7 3
♦ A J
♣ 10 9 6 5

NORTH
WEST   EAST
SOUTH

♠ A K 4
♥ J 8 5 4 2
♦ 4 3
♣ Q 3 2

Suggested Bidding	WEST	NORTH	EAST	SOUTH
	1♦	Pass	1♠	Pass
	2♠	Double	Pass	4♥
	Pass	Pass	Pass	

West opens the bidding 1♦. North, without support for spades, doesn't have the right hand to make a takeout double. With no five-card suit to overcall, North has to settle for a pass at this point.

East, with 5 high-card points plus 1 length point for the five-card suit, has enough to respond 1♠. South's heart suit isn't strong enough to overcall at the two level, especially when vulnerable. South passes, and West raises partner's response to 2♠.

At this point, North can enter the auction with a takeout double. This delayed takeout double shows exactly this type of hand: spade shortness and support for the unbid suits, hearts and clubs. It also implies support for diamonds. With a two-suited hand, North would likely have overcalled at the first opportunity. In effect, North is saying, "I have a takeout double of spades, not a takeout double of diamonds."

After East passes, South has too much to bid 3♥. Bidding at the cheapest level would show 0–8 points . . . no interest in game. Instead, South should jump. This gets the partnership to game, but that should be fine. North was willing to compete to the three level even if South held very little. South has five hearts, a useful fitting card in clubs, and some spade winners. South's 4♥ bid should end the auction.

Suggested Opening Lead

West might lead the ♣Q, top of the touching honors in the suit the partnership has bid and raised, or might choose the ♦10, top of the touching honors from the interior sequence. West will likely settle on the ♣Q.

Suggested Play

Declarer, South, has a spade loser, a heart loser assuming the missing hearts aren't divided 4-0, two diamond losers, and a club loser. Two losers have to be eliminated. The spade loser can be ruffed in dummy, so declarer has to eliminate one of the diamond losers or the club loser.

Since West opened 1♦, South's main chance is that West holds the ♦A. On the actual hand, the diamond finesse doesn't work because East holds the ♦A. Declarer must then avoid a club loser.

When tackling clubs, declarer should not lead the ♣Q because declarer is missing the ♣10 and ♣9. If East holds the ♣K, the ♣Q will lose to the ♣K; if West holds the ♣K, the ♣Q will be covered with the ♣K and declarer will be no better off. Declarer should plan on leading a low club and finessing dummy's ♣J; when that works, declarer can take dummy's ♣A. That works if West holds the singleton or doubleton ♣K . . . as on the actual hand. Declarer's ♣Q becomes a winner[18].

Should declarer play trumps after winning the first spade? As a general guideline, declarer shouldn't draw trumps if there are a lot of other things to do. On this hand, declarer has to ruff a spade loser, lead toward the ♦K, and take a club finesse. Since all of these require entries to the South hand, declarer should do one of them while it is convenient. For example, declarer might ruff the spade loser in dummy at trick two. Now, declarer can start to draw trumps, by leading the ♥K, for example.

Suggested Defense

The defenders can't do anything to prevent declarer from taking ten tricks. If, however, South leads the ♣Q, West must cover with the ♣K to promote East's ♣10 into a winner for the defense.

---

[18] Technically, declarer has an additional chance even if West holds the ♣K and two or more clubs. West will need to keep a high diamond to prevent dummy's diamonds from becoming winners and will have to discard one or more clubs when declarer takes winners in the other suits.

Additional Practice Deals

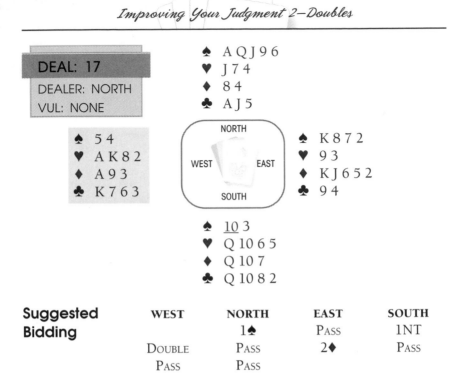

DEAL: 17

DEALER: NORTH
VUL: NONE

♠ A Q J 9 6
♥ J 7 4
♦ 8 4
♣ A J 5

♠ 5 4
♥ A K 8 2
♦ A 9 3
♣ K 7 6 3

NORTH

WEST   EAST

SOUTH

♠ K 8 7 2
♥ 9 3
♦ K J 6 5 2
♣ 9 4

♠ 10 3
♥ Q 10 6 5
♦ Q 10 7
♣ Q 10 8 2

Suggested	WEST	NORTH	EAST	SOUTH
Bidding		1♠	PASS	1NT
	DOUBLE	PASS	2♦	PASS
	PASS	PASS		

North opens 1♠. East passes. South, with 6 high-card points but with-out support for spades, responds 1NT. West can make a takeout double of spades, the only suit bid by the opponents. Although the standard agreement is that a double of a 1NT opening bid is for penalty, the double of a 1NT response is for takeout.

North, with a balanced hand and no extra strength, passes. East takes West's double out to 2♦. With 7 high-card points and a five-card suit, East is close to a jump to 3♦, but should probably take the more conservative approach. If the opponents compete further, East should be willing to take another bid. On the actual layout, East's 2♦ call is likely to end the auction.

Suggested Opening Lead

Against East's 2♦, South leads the ♠10, top of the doubleton in partner's suit.

Suggested Play

After South's opening ♠10 lead, East can take a trick with the ♠K, so there are three spade losers, one diamond loser . . . assuming the missing diamonds break 3-2 . . . and two club losers. There is a total of six losers, one more than East can afford.

East can try to avoid a diamond loser by leading toward the ♦J, hoping it will take a trick. Declarer can also try to avoid a club loser by leading toward the ♣K. A much safer line, however, is to plan to ruff at least one of the spade losers in dummy . . . perhaps both (for an overtrick).

Suppose North wins the first trick with the ♠A and returns the ♠Q. East can win the ♠K and immediately lead a third round of spades, planning to ruff in dummy. East knows that South has no more spades, but that should not matter. If South discards, declarer can ruff with one of West's low trumps. If South chooses to ruff with the ♦10, declarer can overruff with dummy's ♦A.

In either case, declarer can return to the East hand by playing the ♥A-K and ruffing the third round of hearts. Declarer can then lead a fourth round of spades. If South doesn't ruff, declarer ruffs a second spade loser in dummy. If South had ruffed with the ♦10 on the third round of spades, forcing declarer to overruff with dummy's ♦A, South can now ruff the fourth round of spades with the ♦Q and win the trick. That's okay, declarer had to lose a trump trick anyway.

By planning to ruff two spades in dummy before drawing trumps, declarer should lose only one spade, one diamond, and two clubs and make an overtrick.

Suggested Defense

If declarer wins the second round of spades and immediately plays trumps by playing a diamond to dummy's ♦A and then finessing the ♦J on the way back, the contract can be defeated. After winning the ♦Q, South can play a third round of trumps, removing dummy's last trump. Now declarer will lose three spade tricks in addition to the diamond trick and two club tricks.

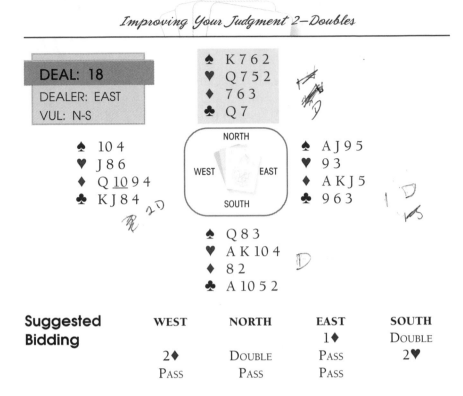

DEAL: 18	♠ K 7 6 2
DEALER: EAST	♥ Q 7 5 2
VUL: N-S	♦ 7 6 3
	♣ Q 7

	♠ A J 9 5
♠ 10 4	♥ 9 3
♥ J 8 6	♦ A K J 5
♦ Q 10 9 4	♣ 9 6 3
♣ K J 8 4	

♠ Q 8 3
♥ A K 10 4
♦ 8 2
♣ A 10 5 2

Suggested	**WEST**	**NORTH**	**EAST**	**SOUTH**
Bidding			1♦	DOUBLE
	2♦	DOUBLE	PASS	2♥
	PASS	PASS	PASS	

East opens 1♦. South has the right type of hand for a takeout double despite having only three-card spade support. West, the responder, with four-card support and 7 high-card points plus 1 dummy point for the doubleton spade, has enough to raise opener to 2♦. By raising, East-West may get to buy the contract or may make the auction more difficult for the opponents.

North, with 7 high-card points, has enough to compete for the contract. Playing standard methods, North will have to guess whether to bid hearts or spades. With both majors, North will probably bid spades, falling back on the general guideline of advancing in the higher-ranking suit. On the actual hand, this won't work out very well since South has only three-card support for spades.

If the partnership has agreed to play responsive doubles, a double of 2♦ by North resolves the dilemma. North's double is for takeout, showing enough to compete and asking South to help choose the best trump suit. Over North's responsive double, South would bid 2♥ and the partnership finds its eight-card fit. With nothing extra, North would pass South's 2♥ bid and settle for partscore.

Suggested Opening Lead

Against South's 2♥ contract, West leads the ♦10, top of the interior sequence in partner's suit.

Suggested Play

Declarer has two spade losers, no heart losers assuming the missing hearts are divided 3-2, two diamond losers, and three club losers. There is a total of seven losers, two more than declarer can afford.

South could plan to ruff two club losers in dummy, but could get overruffed if East has only two or three clubs. A better plan is to lead toward dummy's ♣Q, hoping it will take a trick. That will establish dummy's ♣Q as a winner if West holds the ♣K. Now declarer is left with only one club loser to ruff and can afford to draw trumps.

Suppose the defenders start by leading three rounds of diamonds. South ruffs the third round and leads a low club. If West plays low, dummy's ♣Q will win the trick and declarer can later ruff a club loser in dummy. If West rises with the ♣K, dummy's ♣Q is now established as a winner.

If West wins the ♣K and leads the ♠10, declarer plays low from North. East should also play low, allowing declarer to win a trick with the ♠Q. If East were to play the ♠A, declarer would get tricks with both the ♠K and ♠Q. Declarer can now play a low club to dummy's ♣Q and play three rounds of trumps. Finally, declarer takes the ♣A and ruffs the remaining club loser with dummy's last trump. Declarer loses two spades, two diamonds, and a club.

Suggested Defense

The defenders can't prevent declarer from taking eight tricks in a heart contract if declarer leads toward the ♣Q.

If North-South land in a spade contract, the defenders should get at least six tricks . . . three spade tricks, two diamonds, and a club.

```
DEAL: 19

DEALER: SOUTH
VUL: E-W
```

♠ A 9 8 7 5
♥ A 8
♦ Q 7 6 3
♣ A 2

	NORTH	
♠ K 10 4		♠ Q 2
♥ J 3	WEST EAST	♥ K Q 9 4
♦ 8 5 2		♦ A K J
♣ Q 10 9 7 4	SOUTH	♣ K J 8 6

♠ J 6 3
♥ 10 7 6 5 2
♦ 10 9 4
♣ 5 3

Suggested	WEST	NORTH	EAST	SOUTH
Bidding				PASS
	PASS	1♠	DOUBLE	PASS
	2♣	PASS	2♠	PASS
	2NT	PASS	3NT	PASS
	PASS	PASS		

South and West pass. North opens the bidding 1♠. East, with 19 high-card points, has more than enough for a takeout double. After South passes, West bids 2♣, showing about 0-8 points.

North passes and East has to decide what call to make. East has support for clubs, but a raise to 3♣ would only show an intermediate hand of about 17-18 points and a jump to 4♣ would take the partnership beyond 3NT. To show the strength, East cuebids 2♠. This says nothing about spades. It shows a strong hand with interest in reaching game and asks advancer to make a further descriptive bid.

West has the top of the minimum range with a five-card suit and some strength in spades. Having shown the club suit, West's most descriptive bid is 2NT, showing some strength in spades. East is happy to raise to 3NT. It should be easier to take nine tricks in a notrump than eleven tricks in a minor suit.

Suggested Opening Lead

Against West's 3NT, North would lead the ♠7, fourth highest.

Suggested Play

Declarer, West, starts with only two sure winners, the ♦A-K. By play-ing a low spade from East at trick one, West is guaranteed two tricks in the suit. Declarer can promote four winners in the club suit, leaving one more trick to establish. This can come from promotion in the heart suit or through a successful diamond finesse.

The danger is that North could establish enough spade tricks to defeat the contract before West can establish the winners required. Declarer can't afford to give up the lead too many times.

After North leads the ♠7, declarer plays a low spade from dummy. South plays the ♠J and West wins with the ♠K. Declarer still has the ♠10 and dummy's ♠Q remaining, so there is a second spade trick if the defenders continue to lead spades. Declarer now goes after the club suit, driving out North's ♣A.

Suppose North continues by leading the ♠A and a third round of spades . . . establishing two more winners for the defenders' suit. De-clarer can win the ♠10 and take the club winners but must then decide whether to take the diamond finesse or promote an extra winner in hearts. Promoting a heart would be surer than the 50-50 diamond fi-nesse, but declarer can't afford to let North regain the lead. North would then take two spade winners and defeat the contract. Declarer must rely on the diamond finesse which, if successful, won't give up the lead.

Declarer must keep this option available when discarding from dummy on the third round of spades and fifth round of clubs. De-clarer must keep dummy's ♦J and, instead, discard two hearts from the dummy. Declarer will then be in a position to take the diamond finesse. On the actual hand, North holds the ♦Q, so all is well. De-clarer takes nine tricks: two spades, three diamonds, and four clubs.

Suggested Defense

North's best defense is to continue leading spades, establishing the two extra winners in that suit. North will have to discard when de-clarer takes the established club winners and should not discard a spade. Instead North should discard the ♥8 and two low diamonds. If declarer then tries to establish a heart winner, North will be able to win the ♥A and take enough tricks to defeat the contract. Discarding the diamonds can't hurt since declarer could always take the diamond finesse if declarer chooses that line of play.

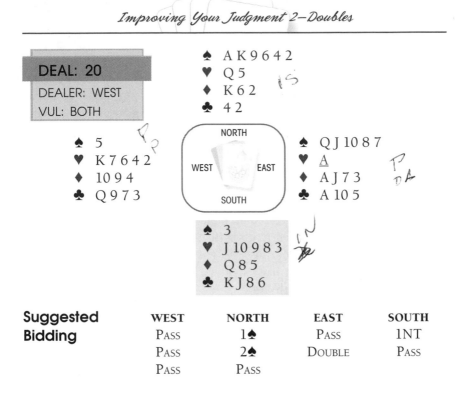

DEAL: 20
DEALER: WEST
VUL: BOTH

NORTH
♠ A K 9 6 4 2
♥ Q 5
♦ K 6 2
♣ 4 2

WEST
♠ 5
♥ K 7 6 4 2
♦ 10 9 4
♣ Q 9 7 3

EAST
♠ Q J 10 8 7
♥ A
♦ A J 7 3
♣ A 10 5

SOUTH
♠ 3
♥ J 10 9 8 3
♦ Q 8 5
♣ K J 8 6

Suggested
Bidding

WEST	NORTH	EAST	SOUTH
PASS	1♠	PASS	1NT
PASS	2♠	DOUBLE	PASS
PASS	PASS		

West passes. North has 12 high-card points plus 2 length points for the six-card suit. That makes the hand too strong for a weak 2♠ bid. Instead, North opens 1♠. East has a good hand but no suitable action over 1♠. East doesn't have the right shape for a takeout double and doesn't have a five-card or longer suit to overcall. Also, with an unbalanced hand, a 1NT overcall isn't a good choice. East should simply pass and await developments.

South has enough to respond 1NT and West passes. With a six-card suit, North rebids 2♠. At this point, East can come into the auction with a penalty double. East's double is not for takeout. East is not in the balancing position and, if East had wanted to make a takeout double of spades, East would have doubled 1♠.

South may suspect that the partnership is in trouble but has no reason to disturb the contract. Bidding 2NT or 3♥ may get the partnership to a worse spot. South should probably pass. West should also pass, since East's double is for penalty, not for takeout. North has nowhere to go, so the contract should end in 2♠ doubled.

Suggested Opening Lead

Against North's 2♠ doubled contract, East has a choice of leads and might start with the ♠Q . . . a safe lead that should give nothing away . . . or the ♥A, hoping to ruff hearts later on.

Suggested Play

2♠ is not a pleasant contract for North. Declarer could hope that the missing spades are divided 3-3, so there is only one loser in that suit. If the contract has been doubled, however, North can expect that the missing spades are divided 4-2 or worse. In addition, there are two heart losers, two diamond losers, and two club losers. That's at least eight losers . . . three too many. North's plan should be to take tricks any way possible.

Suppose East leads the ♥A and then switches to the ♠Q . . . the best defense. North should win the ♠K and immediately lead a club. If East plays low (best), declarer will have to guess to play dummy's ♣K, to win the trick. North should then lead a second club, hoping to eventually ruff a club. Ruffing in declarer's hand and scoring a small trump may gain a trick when the trumps are badly divided.

Declarer can lead to dummy's ♦Q, and hope that East is later forced to lead diamonds, so that declarer gets a second trick with the ♦K. That way, declarer could take five or six tricks. Unfortunately for declarer, the 2♠ contract is destined to be defeated at least two tricks, if not more.

Suggested Defense

East should get at least three spade tricks and the three aces. In addition, West should get a trick with the ♥K and, perhaps the ♣Q. The defenders may even get two diamond tricks if declarer has to play that suit. All roads should lead to a defeat of 2♠ by at least two tricks . . . more likely three tricks.

West does well not to takeout the penalty double. West would not fare well in a heart contract and East-West cannot make a notrump contract if the defenders lead hearts early on.

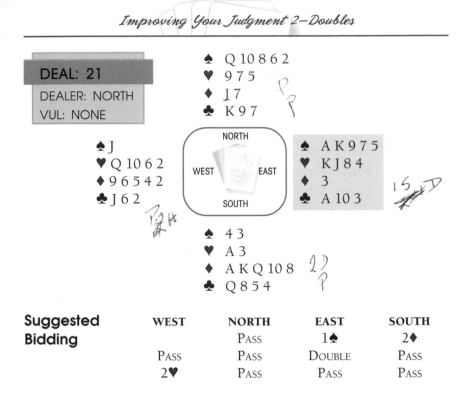

				NORTH
		♠ Q 10 8 6 2		
		♥ 9 7 5		
		♦ J 7		
		♣ K 9 7		

DEAL: 21

DEALER: NORTH
VUL: NONE

WEST
♠ J
♥ Q 10 6 2
♦ 9 6 5 4 2
♣ J 6 2

EAST
♠ A K 9 7 5
♥ K J 8 4
♦ 3
♣ A 10 3

SOUTH
♠ 4 3
♥ A 3
♦ A K Q 10 8
♣ Q 8 5 4

Suggested Bidding	**WEST**	**NORTH**	**EAST**	**SOUTH**
		PASS	1♠	2♦
	PASS	PASS	DOUBLE	PASS
	2♥	PASS	PASS	PASS

North passes. East opens 1♠. South has a sound hand for an overcall of 2♦. West doesn't have enough to take any action at this point and neither does North.

The auction comes back to East who has too much to let the opponents play the contract in 2♦. With shortness in diamonds, East can reopen the bidding with a takeout double. East has already promised a five-card spade suit. The double shows interest in competing in one of the unbid suits, hearts or clubs. If West doesn't have a fit with either of those suits, West could return to East's known five-card spade suit, bid notrump, or convert the double into a penalty double by passing[19].

After South passes, West takes the double out to 2♥. Although West has five diamonds, they are not very high so West should not consider passing for penalties. In fact, South can make 2♦. West's 2♥ call should end the auction.

---

[19] If the partnership plays negative doubles, a double by West of the 2♦ overcall would be for takeout. To make a penalty double of 2♦, West would have to pass and wait for East to reopen with a double.

Suggested Opening Lead

Against West's 2♥ contract, North would lead the ♦J, top of the doubleton in partner's suit.

Suggested Play

Declarer has a heart loser, five diamond losers, and two club losers . . . a total of eight losers. That's three too many. Declarer can plan to discard one of the losers on the extra spade winner in dummy and ruff at least two diamond losers in the dummy. This means declarer can't afford to draw trumps.

Suppose South wins the first diamond trick and, seeing that declarer will probably want to ruff diamond losers in dummy, plays the ♥A and a second round of hearts. Declarer can win the second round of hearts in the West hand and lead a diamond, ruffing in dummy. Declarer can take dummy's ♠A and ♠K discarding either a club or a diamond loser from the West hand. To get back to the West hand, declarer can lead a third round of spades and ruff in the West hand. Declarer can then lead another diamond and ruff with dummy's remaining trump. Declarer can take a trick with the ♣A and still has a high trump in the West hand. That's eight tricks.

Suggested Defense

After North leads a diamond, the defenders can limit declarer to eight tricks by playing two rounds of trumps. South is looking at all the high diamonds and can see the singleton in dummy. So, South should overtake the first diamond and play the ♥A and a second heart. If the defenders don't lead hearts early, declarer may make at least nine tricks by ruffing three . . . or even four . . . diamond losers in the dummy.

To defeat 2♥, North would have to find the lead of a trump. South wins the ♥A and plays a second round. When declarer leads a diamond, North must win with the ♦J and play a third round of trumps . . . a very difficult defense!

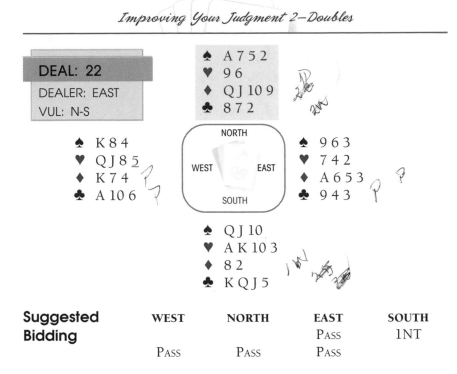

DEAL: 22	♠ A 7 5 2
DEALER: EAST	♥ 9 6
VUL: N-S	♦ Q J 10 9
	♣ 8 7 2

NORTH

WEST	EAST
♠ K 8 4	♠ 9 6 3
♥ Q J 8 5	♥ 7 4 2
♦ K 7 4	♦ A 6 5 3
♣ A 10 6	♣ 9 4 3

SOUTH

♠ Q J 10
♥ A K 10 3
♦ 8 2
♣ K Q J 5

Suggested Bidding

WEST	NORTH	EAST	SOUTH
		PASS	1NT
PASS	PASS	PASS	

East passes. South, with a balanced hand and 16 high-card points, opens the bidding 1NT. West has 13 high-card points and support for all four unbid suits. The standard agreement, however, is that a direct double of a 1NT opening bid is for penalty, not for takeout. In general, it's dangerous to come into the auction with a balanced hand when the opponent on your right has shown a strong balanced hand and the opponent on your left could have values. Bidding over an opponent's opening 1NT bid is usually safer with an unbalanced hand.

If West passes, North would also pass. North has a balanced hand with 7 high-card points. North doesn't expect the partnership to make more than a partscore, even if opener has a maximum. East will be content to let North-South play in 1NT.

If West does double the 1NT opening bid, East-West will get into trouble. If the double is left in, North-South will make the contract with at least a couple of overtricks. North might even redouble. Holding 7 high-card points, North knows the partnership holds the majority of points and should make at least 1NT.

If East takes the double out to 2♦, North should make a penalty double when the auction comes back around. North is looking at three defensive tricks . . . the ♠A and two diamond tricks . . . and should expect to defeat 2♦ several tricks opposite South's 1NT opening bid.

Even if North-South don't double 2♦, any action by East-West may push North-South into 3NT . . . a game they normally wouldn't reach.

Suggested Opening Lead

Against 1NT, West would start with the ♥5, fourth from longest and strongest.

Suggested Play

Declarer should have little trouble taking at least nine tricks in a notrump contract. If West leads a low heart, declarer will get three tricks in that suit. Declarer can promote two winners in clubs and will get a third trick when the defenders' clubs divide 3-3. Declarer can also get at least three tricks from the spade suit with the help of a successful finesse against West's ♠K.

Suggested Defense

There is no defense to hold declarer to fewer than nine tricks in a notrump contract. In practice, declarer is likely to take ten tricks . . . limiting East-West to the ♦A-K and ♣A.

If East-West get into a diamond contract, it is unlikely they will be able to take more than four tricks . . . the ♦A-K, the ♣A, and perhaps a heart or another diamond trick. In 2♦ doubled, for example, North-South can collect a penalty of 800 points, even though East-West are non vulnerable.

		♠ 2
DEAL: 23		♥ Q J 9 7 6
DEALER: SOUTH		♦ 8 5
VUL: E-W		♣ 10 8 7 5 3

	NORTH	
♠ K Q J 9		♠ A 8 7 3
♥ 2	WEST EAST	♥ 5 3
♦ K Q J 3		♦ A 9 7 4 2
♣ 9 6 4 2	SOUTH	♣ Q J

	♠ 10 6 5 4
	♥ A K 10 8 4
	♦ 10 6
	♣ A K

Suggested Bidding

WEST	NORTH	EAST	SOUTH
			1♥
DOUBLE	4♥	4♠	PASS
PASS	PASS		

After South opens 1♥, West has the right strength and shape for a takeout double. Over the double, North should make a preemptive jump raise to 4♥. This shows a weak hand and five-card support. Because of the strong support and good distribution, North doesn't expect to be heavily penalized if the opponents choose to double 4♥. If 4♥ is defeated, it is likely that East-West can make a game.

Over North's jump to 4♥, East has to decide what to do. With 11 high-card points and a five-card suit, it is likely that East-West can make game. Although East has a five-card diamond suit, it is more practical to bid 4♠. Partner probably has four-card spade support for the double and a contract of 4♠ requires one less trick than 5♦.

East's other option is to make a penalty double of 4♥. However, there is no guarantee that 4♥ will be defeated. Even if it can be defeated, the penalty may not be sufficient compensation for game.

East's 4♠ bid will probably end the auction, although South might consider making a *sacrifice* bid of 5♥. South, however, has a good hand for defense, although not good enough to double for penalty opposite partner's preemptive raise. South has four trumps and the

♣A-K and ♥A are likely to take tricks. South doesn't need much from partner to defeat the contract.

Suggested Opening Lead

Against 4♠ South could lead the ♥A, top of the touching high cards in the partnership suit. Another choice might be to lead the ♣K and ♣A[20], hoping to get a ruff in that suit (see below).

Suggested Play

East has two heart losers and two club losers, one too many. One heart can be ruffed in dummy, so the contract appears secure provided the missing trumps are divided 3-2. On the actual hand, however, the 4-1 trump division provides a challenge.

Suppose South wins the first heart, takes the top two clubs, and plays a second heart. Declarer ruffs in dummy with the ♠9 and starts to draw trumps by playing the ♠K-Q, discovering the 4-1 division. Declarer can't afford to overtake dummy's ♠J, since that would establish South's ♠10 as a winner. Instead, declarer must take dummy's ♠J and cross to the East hand with the ♦A to draw South's last trump.

When crossing to the East hand, declarer has to lead a high diamond, not the ♦3, and overtake with the ♦A. Declarer can then draw South's last trump and take West's remaining high diamonds. Finally, declarer leads the carefully preserved ♦3 to get back to the last two diamonds in the East hand. If declarer doesn't lead a high diamond over to the ♦A, declarer won't be able to take all five diamond winners.

Suggested Defense

As discussed above, South can't defeat the contract by taking the ♥A and ♣A-K and then leading another heart. A more challenging defense is to start by playing the ♣A-K and then leading a low heart to put North on lead. North can then lead a third round of clubs. If declarer ruffs low, South can overruff to defeat the contract.

Declarer can counter this defense by ruffing with the ♠A, then taking two rounds of trumps with dummy's ♠K-Q, discovering the bad break. Declarer can cross to the ♦A . . . playing one of dummy's high diamonds, as above . . . and lead a spade to finesse against South's ♠10.

[20] If the partnership normally leads the ace from a suit headed by the ace-king, the lead of the king followed by the ace specifically shows a doubleton.

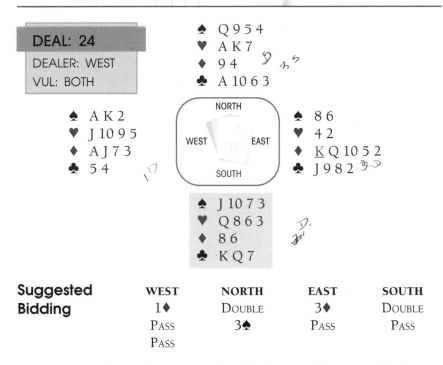

DEAL: 24
DEALER: WEST
VUL: BOTH

NORTH
♠ Q 9 5 4
♥ A K 7
♦ 9 4
♣ A 10 6 3

WEST
♠ A K 2
♥ J 10 9 5
♦ A J 7 3
♣ 5 4

EAST
♠ 8 6
♥ 4 2
♦ K Q 10 5 2
♣ J 9 8 2

SOUTH
♠ J 10 7 3
♥ Q 8 6 3
♦ 8 6
♣ K Q 7

Suggested Bidding

WEST	NORTH	EAST	SOUTH
1♦	DOUBLE	3♦	DOUBLE
PASS	3♠	PASS	PASS
PASS			

West opens 1♦. North, even with only three-card support for hearts, has the right hand for a takeout double. Over the takeout double, East can make a preemptive jump raise to 3♦. After a takeout double, a jump raise is weak, not invitational. With 10 or more points, East could start with a redouble[21]. The advantage of the preemptive jump is that it makes it more difficult for the opponents to find their best contract.

If East does jump to 3♦, South faces a challenge. South has 8 high-card points, enough to compete, but can't be sure which suit to bid. South doesn't want to land in a seven-card fit at the three level. This dilemma is solved if the partnership agrees to use responsive doubles. Playing this convention, a double by advancer after responder's raise of opener's suit to the two or three level is for takeout, not for penalty. It shows interest in competing in one of the majors.

Over South's responsive double, North bids four-card suits up the line, looking for a fit. On this hand, North would bid 3♠. Having found a fit, South is happy to settle for partscore and passes.

[21] With a club fit and enough for a limit raise, some partnerships use a conventional 2NT in place of the redouble.

Suggested Opening Lead

Against 3♠ by North, East would lead the ♦K, top of the broken sequence in the partnership's suit.

Suggested Play

Declarer has two spade losers, two diamond losers, and a club loser . . . one too many. North's primary focus should be on drawing spades as soon as possible to prevent the defenders from ruffing any of the heart or club winners (see below). If the ♣J doesn't fall, declarer can ruff the club loser in the dummy after trumps have been drawn.

For example, suppose East wins the first two diamond tricks with the ♦K and ♦Q and leads a heart. Declarer should win and immediately lead a spade. West can win the ♠K and lead a second heart, but declarer wins and leads a second round of trumps, driving out West's ♠A. Luckily for declarer, if West leads a third round of hearts, East has no trump left with which to ruff. Declarer can draw West's last trump and then ruff the club loser in dummy.

Suggested Defense

After the lead of the ♦K, West can see that the defenders have two spade tricks and two diamond tricks . . . if declarer doesn't have a singleton diamond. West can try for a fifth defensive trick by getting a club ruff. Since West will need an entry to the East hand in the diamond suit to get a club ruff, West should overtake the ♦K with the ♦A and immediately lead a club. If declarer leads a spade[22], West can win the ♠K and lead a second club. If declarer leads another spade, West can win the ♠A and then return a diamond to East's ♦Q. East can top off a fine defense by leading a third round of clubs for West to ruff.

If North-South play in a heart contract instead of a spade contract, the defenders can limit declarer to seven tricks. They can take two diamond tricks, two spade tricks and a spade ruff in the East hand, plus an eventual heart trick by West.

If East-West are left to play in a diamond partscore, they can take nine tricks. West can ruff a spade and two heart losers in the dummy. The only tricks East-West lose are two hearts and two clubs.

---

[22] Declarer can spoil West's plan by leading a diamond after winning the first club. This is a far-sighted play to remove the entry to the East hand.

	♠ 8 4
DEAL: 25	♥ K 10 8 3
DEALER: NORTH	♦ Q 6 2
VUL: NONE	♣ Q 10 7 4

```
                    NORTH
♠ 9 7 5                          ♠ K Q J 2
♥ Q 9 6 5      WEST      EAST    ♥ 7 4 2
♦ 10 3                           ♦ A J 9 7 4
♣ 8 6 5 2                        ♣ J
                    SOUTH
```

♠ A 10 6 3
♥ A J
♦ K 8 5
♣ A K 9 3

Suggested	WEST	NORTH	EAST	SOUTH
Bidding		PASS	1♦	DOUBLE
	PASS	1♥	PASS	1NT
	PASS	3NT	PASS	PASS
	PASS			

After North passes, East opens the bidding with 1♦. South has 19 high-card points, too much for a simple overcall of 1NT. With a hand too strong to overcall, South starts with a takeout double. North assumes it is a standard takeout double and, after West passes, bids 1♥. With a choice between clubs and hearts, North prefers the major . . . it can be bid at a cheaper level and the score for a major suit is worth more than the score for a minor suit.

After East passes, South rebids 1NT. By doubling and bidding notrump, South is showing a hand too strong for a direct overcall of 1NT, about 19 to 21 points. With 7 high-card points, North now has enough to raise to the game level.

If South had overcalled 1NT originally, showing 15-18 points, North would probably have passed and the partnership would not reach the game contract.

Suggested Opening Lead

West is on lead against South's 3NT and should lead partner's suit, the ♦10, top of a doubleton.

Suggested Play

Declarer will get a diamond trick after the opening lead and has a sure trick in spades, two sure tricks in hearts, and four sure tricks in clubs if the suit divides 3-2 or the ♣J can be found. That leaves one more trick to develop. It should be possible to develop an extra trick in the heart suit, either with the help of a finesse or through promotion since North-South have both the ♥J and ♥10. However, declarer must be careful when developing a trick in hearts.

If East lets declarer win the first trick with the ♦K, then West becomes the dangerous opponent. If West gains the lead, West could lead another diamond, trapping North's ♦Q. If East gets the lead, there is no danger. East can't lead diamonds without giving declarer a second trick with dummy's ♦Q. That tells declarer how to play the heart suit.

After winning the ♦K, declarer should lead the ♥A and then the ♥J, playing a low heart from dummy if West doesn't cover with the ♥Q. That guarantees the contract. On the actual lie of the cards, the ♥J will win and declarer has nine tricks . . . one spade, three hearts, one diamond, and four clubs. Even if East held the ♥Q, the contract would still be safe. East can't profitably lead a diamond and declarer now has two established heart winners in dummy, the ♥K and ♥10 to go with the other winners.

Suggested Defense

When West leads the ♦10 and declarer plays a low card from dummy, East should not play the ♦A. That would give declarer two tricks with the ♦K and ♦Q. Instead, East should make an encouraging signal with the ♦7, keeping dummy's ♦Q trapped.

If declarer crosses to dummy with a club winner and takes a finesse by playing a low heart to the ♥J, the defenders can defeat the contract. West wins the ♥Q and can lead a second diamond. The defenders can now take four diamond tricks to defeat the contract.

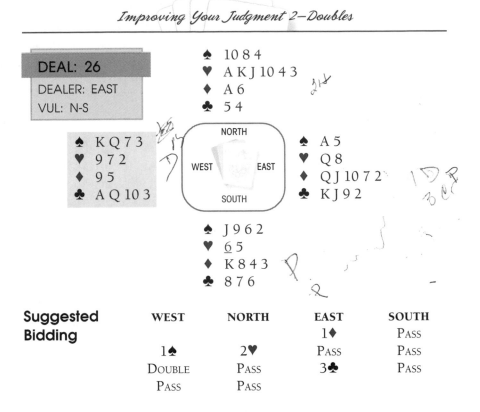

DEAL: 26
DEALER: EAST
VUL: N-S

NORTH
♠ 10 8 4
♥ A K J 10 4 3
♦ A 6
♣ 5 4

WEST
♠ K Q 7 3
♥ 9 7 2
♦ 9 5
♣ A Q 10 3

EAST
♠ A 5
♥ Q 8
♦ Q J 10 7 2
♣ K J 9 2

SOUTH
♠ J 9 6 2
♥ 6 5
♦ K 8 4 3
♣ 8 7 6

Suggested Bidding

WEST	NORTH	EAST	SOUTH
		1♦	PASS
1♠	2♥	PASS	PASS
DOUBLE	PASS	3♣	PASS
PASS	PASS		

East opens the longer minor. South passes. West, looking for a major suit fit, responds 1♠. North enters the auction with an overcall of 2♥. East, with a minimum opening and only two spades, should pass at this point. South also passes, and the bidding comes back to West.

With 11 high-card points, West has too much to let North buy the contract for 2♥ and can show willingness to compete further by making a reopening double. The double is not for penalty. It sends the message to East that the partnership has the majority of the strength but that West doesn't have a better choice of call. West doesn't have a long spade suit which can be rebid and doesn't have good support for opener's first bid suit, diamonds. The double lets East decide on the best action for the partnership, including passing and converting the takeout double into a penalty double.

On the actual hand, East doesn't have good defense against 2♥ and can now show the second suit by bidding 3♣. East isn't promising any extra strength by going to the three level. With a good hand, East would have bid 3♣ directly over North's 2♥ bid. West is happy to settle for partscore in clubs. North may be tempted to bid again but should pass since it sounds as though East-West have the balance of power.

Suggested Opening Lead

Against 3♣, South leads the ♥6, top of the doubleton in partner's suit.

Suggested Play

Declarer has two heart losers and two diamond losers. The hand might seem straightforward, however, declarer needs to maintain control of the trump suit and watch the entries. Declarer can plan to promote the winners in the diamond suit, keeping the ♠A as an entry.

Suppose North wins the first two heart tricks and leads a third round. East must ruff high because otherwise South can overruff. East should then lead a diamond, driving out one of the defenders' high diamonds before drawing trumps (it doesn't actually matter on the lie of the cards). If the defender who wins the first diamond returns a spade, declarer should win in the West hand, keeping the ♠A as an entry to the long diamonds. After regaining the lead, declarer can draw trumps and drive out the remaining high diamond[23].

Declarer loses two hearts and two diamonds.

Suggested Defense

There's nothing the defenders can do to prevent East-West from taking nine tricks in clubs if declarer plays the hand correctly.

North can be defeated in a 2♥ contract, but only with perfect defense. The defenders must take exactly two club winners and then three spade winners, ending in the West hand. West can then lead a fourth round of spades and East will get a trick with the ♥Q whether North ruffs high or low. If the defenders start with four rounds of spades, North can discard a club loser on the fourth round, letting East ruff. Declarer will later drop East's ♥Q. Declarer gets six heart tricks and two diamond tricks. If East leads a diamond initially, declarer can make the contract by guessing to play the ♥A-K, dropping East's ♥Q.

---

[23] A slightly easier line of play is for declarer to play the ♠A, ♠K, and lead a low spade and ruff in the East hand. Then declarer plays the ♣K and a low club to the West hand to draw the remaining trumps. This is a dummy reversal.

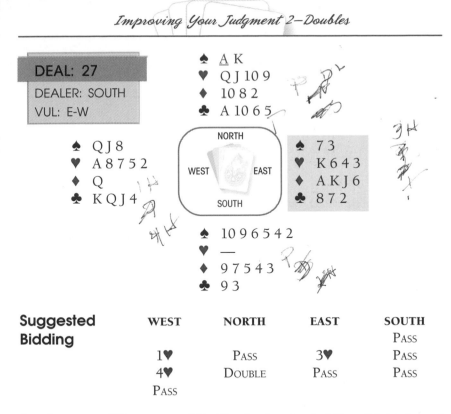

	NORTH		
	♠ A K		
	♥ Q J 10 9		
	♦ 10 8 2		
	♣ A 10 6 5		

DEAL: 27
DEALER: SOUTH
VUL: E-W

WEST
♠ Q J 8
♥ A 8 7 5 2
♦ Q
♣ K Q J 4

EAST
♠ 7 3
♥ K 6 4 3
♦ A K J 6
♣ 8 7 2

SOUTH
♠ 10 9 6 5 4 2
♥ —
♦ 9 7 5 4 3
♣ 9 3

Suggested Bidding

WEST	NORTH	EAST	SOUTH
			Pass
1♥	Pass	3♥	Pass
4♥	Double	Pass	Pass
Pass			

South passes. West opens 1♥. North, despite holding 14 high-card points, doesn't have any suitable competitive action over West's opening bid. North doesn't have a five-card suit to overcall and doesn't have the required spade support to make a takeout double. The best action is to pass and await developments.

East, with 11 high-card points and 1 dummy point for the doubleton spade, has enough for a limit raise of 3♥, inviting opener to bid game. South passes. West, with 15 high-card points and a five-card suit, has enough to accept.

When West bids 4♥, North can now enter the auction with a penalty double. North has two sure tricks in the trump suit and three likely side tricks: the ♠A-K and ♣A.

Although South has a shapely hand with no defense against a heart contract, South should pass partner's penalty double. If North had wanted to make a takeout double of hearts, North would have doubled 1♥ instead of waiting until the opponents reached a game. South shouldn't overrule partner's decision to defend for penalties.

Suggested Opening Lead

Against West's 4♥ doubled, North would start with the ♠A or ♠K. It is possible that a trump lead might be best . . . if dummy has a singleton spade, for example . . . but it is also possible that declarer may be able to discard spade losers if North doesn't take the winners in that suit right away.

Suggested Play

If North takes the ♠A-K and ♣A right away, there is nothing declarer can do[24]. With the unfortunate 4-0 break in hearts, declarer also has two heart losers.

Suggested Defense

North can simply take the three winners outside the heart suit and sit back to collect the two heart winners.

East-West should not be discouraged if the 4♥ contract is doubled and defeated two tricks. They were unlucky to get a 4-0 trump split. If the missing trumps were divided 2-2, the contract would make. Even if the missing trumps were divided 3-1, it is unlikely they would be doubled. Unlucky.

If South does take out North's penalty double, East-West will have a chance to turn the tables. 4♠ doubled can be defeated three tricks . . . one spade trick, four diamonds, and a club.

---

[24] If North leads the ♥Q, declarer may make the contract. Declarer can win the ♥A, play the ♦Q, then cross to dummy with the ♥K. Declarer can then play the ♦A-K-J, discarding the three spade losers from the West hand. If North ruffs the last diamond, declarer can eventually ruff a club loser in dummy. To defeat the contract, North has to refuse to ruff the fourth round of diamonds, discarding a spade winner. On winning the ♣A, North can then draw dummy's remaining trumps and will eventually get the setting trick with the ♣10.

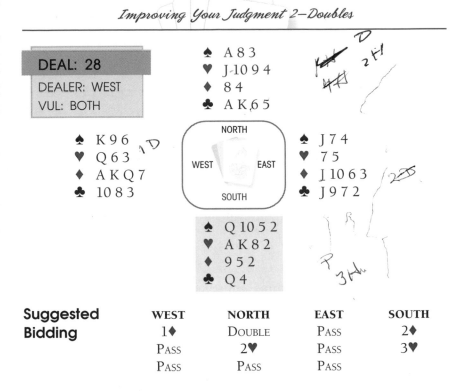

DEAL: 28
DEALER: WEST
VUL: BOTH

NORTH
- ♠ A 8 3
- ♥ J 10 9 4
- ♦ 8 4
- ♣ A K 6 5

WEST
- ♠ K 9 6
- ♥ Q 6 3
- ♦ A K Q 7
- ♣ 10 8 3

EAST
- ♠ J 7 4
- ♥ 7 5
- ♦ J 10 6 3
- ♣ J 9 7 2

SOUTH
- ♠ Q 10 5 2
- ♥ A K 8 2
- ♦ 9 5 2
- ♣ Q 4

Suggested Bidding	**WEST**	**NORTH**	**EAST**	**SOUTH**
	1♦	DOUBLE	PASS	2♦
	PASS	2♥	PASS	3♥
	PASS	PASS	PASS	

After West's opening 1♦ bid, North can make a takeout double. North has support for the unbid suits and 12 high-card points plus 1 dummy point for the doubleton diamond. East doesn't have quite enough to raise to 2♦.

South has 11 high-card points, enough to make an invitational jump. With four-card support for both majors, South would like to land in an eight-card fit. Instead of guessing which major to bid, South can start with a cuebid of 2♦. This is forcing, asking for further information from partner.

In reply to South's cuebid, North bids 2♥, biding four-card suits up the line, looking for a fit. Having found a fit, South can now show a hand of invitational strength by raising to 3♥. North, with a minimum for the takeout double, passes the invitation and settles for partscore.

Suggested Opening Lead

Against North's 3♥, East would lead the ♦J, top of the touching honors in partner's suit.

Suggested Play

Declarer has two spade losers, a heart loser, two diamond losers, and a club loser. Two losers have to be eliminated. The club loser can eventually be ruffed in dummy. Declarer has to get rid of the heart loser or one of the spade losers. North can try the heart finesse, hoping East holds the ♥Q. On the actual hand, the heart finesse doesn't work, so declarer must resort to a spade finesse. In the spade suit, declarer has the option of finessing against the ♠K in the East hand by leading toward dummy's ♠Q, or by finessing against the ♠J in the East hand by leading toward dummy's ♠10. Since West opened the bidding and is likely to hold the ♠K, finessing against the ♠J in the East hand is a better choice.

For example, suppose the defenders start by leading three rounds of diamonds. Declarer ruffs the third round and leads the ♥J, trying the heart finesse. This loses to West's ♥Q and West returns a club. Declarer wins the ♣Q in dummy and draws the remaining trumps. Now declarer takes the ♠A and leads a spade toward dummy. When East plays low, declarer finesses dummy's ♠10. Since East holds the ♠J, West is forced to win this trick with the ♠K. Now dummy's ♠Q has become a winner and declarer can take the remaining tricks. Declarer loses one spade, one heart, and two diamond tricks.

Suggested Defense

East got off to a good start by leading partner's suit. During the play, West should avoid leading a spade because then declarer won't have to guess the spades. The defenders should let declarer play the spade suit. If declarer misguesses, the defenders will be able to take two spade tricks, one heart, and two diamond tricks, to defeat the contract.

DEAL: 29

DEALER: NORTH
VUL: NONE

NORTH
- ♠ 9 7 6
- ♥ A K 7 6 5 3
- ♦ Q J
- ♣ J 10

WEST
- ♠ A K J 4
- ♥ Q J 8 5
- ♦ 8 6 2
- ♣ 8 5 3

EAST
- ♠ Q 10 5 2
- ♥ 4
- ♦ A K 7 3
- ♣ K 6 4 2

SOUTH
- ♠ 8 3
- ♥ 10 9 2
- ♦ 10 9 5 4
- ♣ A Q 9 7

Suggested Bidding

WEST	NORTH	EAST	SOUTH
	1♥	DOUBLE	2♥
2♠	PASS	PASS	PASS

North, with 11 high-card points plus 2 length points, has enough to open the bidding 1♥. The hand is a little too strong for a weak two-bid in hearts. East makes a takeout double with 12 high-card points plus 3 dummy points for the singleton heart. South, with three-card support and 6 high-card points plus 1 dummy point for the doubleton spade, has enough to raise to the two level.

West has 11 high-card points, but should not overvalue the hand. 11 points would normally be enough to make an invitational jump to 3♠ but the ♥Q-J are likely to be wasted values opposite East's shortness in the suit. They would be more valuable in the unbid suits . . . working together with partner's high cards in those suits. West should discount the ♥Q and ♥J and value the hand as only 8 high-card points, enough to compete to 2♠ but not enough to jump to 3♠.

West's 2♠ call will likely end the auction although North might consider bidding 3♥ with the six-card suit.

Suggested Opening Lead

Against West's 2♠, North would lead the ♥A, top of the touching high cards in the partnership's suit.

Suggested Play

Declarer has three heart losers, a diamond loser, and three club losers . . . two more than declarer can afford. There are a number of possibilities. Two heart losers can be ruffed in the dummy. Declarer can try the club finesse, hoping North holds the ♣A. Declarer might also try to establish an extra diamond winner or an extra club winner in dummy if either suit is divided 3-3. The extra winner could then be used to discard a loser from the other minor suit.

On the actual hand, the club finesse doesn't work and both minor suits are divided 4-2, so an extra winner cannot be developed in either suit. There are many ways in which the play might go, but here is a typical example.

Suppose North takes the ♥A and leads the ♦Q. Declarer wins the ♦K and plays a spade to the West hand and leads the ♥Q and ruffs it[25]. Declarer comes back to the West hand with another trump and leads the ♥J and ruffs with dummy's last trump. Declarer now plays the ♦A and leads a third round of diamonds. South wins the ♦9 and may continue with the ♦10. On this trick, West should discard one of the club losers to avoid getting overruffed. Now South will have to play the ♣A and lead a second club. If North has discarded one or more clubs, North will be able to ruff this trick, but that's all for the defense. If declarer is allowed to win dummy's ♣K, then declarer again has eight tricks.

Suggested Defense

After winning the first trick with the ♥A, North can shift to the ♣J, hoping to trap dummy's ♣K. That works well and the defenders can take three club tricks. Eventually, the defenders should also get a diamond trick, holding declarer to eight tricks.

East-West can't afford to get too high on this hand, since they can only take eight tricks in a spade contract. West must avoid getting too high with the 11 "points" opposite partner's takeout double. If North-South push on to 3♥, East-West can get a plus score by choosing to defend. They should take two spades, one heart, and two diamonds on defense.

---

[25] Declarer may not have to ruff both heart losers in dummy if North covers the ♥Q with the ♥K because the ♥J is now a winner.

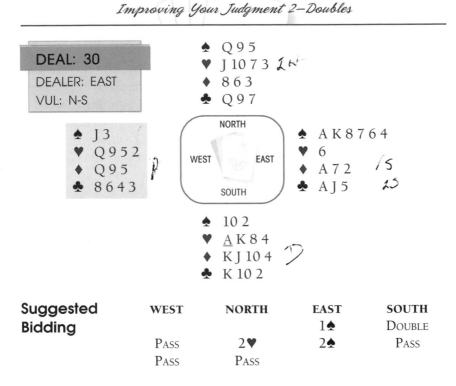

	♠ Q 9 5		
	♥ J 10 7 3		
DEAL: 30	♦ 8 6 3		
DEALER: EAST	♣ Q 9 7		
VUL: N-S			

♠ J 3
♥ Q 9 5 2
♦ Q 9 5
♣ 8 6 4 3

NORTH
WEST · EAST
SOUTH

♠ A K 8 7 6 4
♥ 6
♦ A 7 2
♣ A J 5

♠ 10 2
♥ A K 8 4
♦ K J 10 4
♣ K 10 2

Suggested Bidding

WEST	NORTH	EAST	SOUTH
		1♠	DOUBLE
PASS	2♥	2♠	PASS
PASS	PASS		

East, with 16 high-card points plus 2 length points for the six-card suit, opens 1♠. South, with support for the unbid suits and 14 high-card points plus 1 dummy point for the doubleton spade, makes a takeout double. West, with 5 high-card points and only a doubleton spade, passes. North takes out the double by bidding the four-card suit at the cheapest level, 2♥.

East has a medium-strength hand and would have jumped to 3♠ if West had responded 1NT, for example. Once West passes, East must be more cautious since North-South might have the balance of strength. East can simply rebid 2♠. By bidding a second time with no encouragement from partner, East is showing a good hand.

South, with a minimum takeout double, should now pass. It is tempting to bid again, but South has already described the hand with the takeout double and is in the minimum range. Any further action should be left to North, the advancer, who was forced to bid and could have no points. Advancer will have another chance to compete when holding 6 or more points.

On the actual hand, East's 2♠ should end the auction. North doesn't have enough to want to compete to the three level.

Suggested Opening Lead

Against East's 2♠ contract South would lead the ♥A, top of the touching cards in the partnership's suit.

Suggested Play

If the missing spades divide 3-2, declarer has a spade loser, a heart loser, two diamond losers, and two club losers. That's one too many. Declarer can plan to eliminate one of the diamond losers by taking a finesse. After trumps have been drawn, declarer can play the ♦A and lead toward dummy's ♦Q. The finesse is quite likely to succeed since South made a takeout double and should have most of the missing strength.

On the actual lie of the cards, declarer loses one spade, one heart, one diamond, and two clubs.

Suggested Defense

There is nothing the defenders can do to prevent declarer from taking eight tricks in a spade contract.

If South were to bid 3♥, North-South would be much too high. Since North-South are vulnerable, going down two or three tricks will be expensive, even if the opponents don't double. It will not be a good result since East-West can only make a partscore.

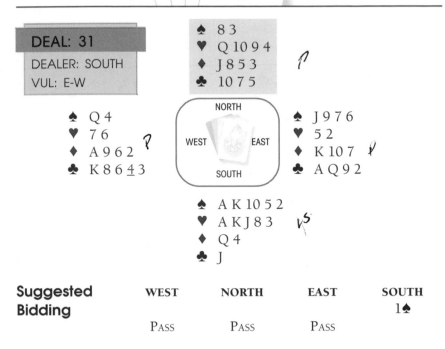

DEAL: 31

DEALER: SOUTH
VUL: E-W

NORTH: ♠ 8 3 ♥ Q 10 9 4 ♦ J 8 5 3 ♣ 10 7 5

WEST: ♠ Q 4 ♥ 7 6 ♦ A 9 6 2 ♣ K 8 6 4 3

EAST: ♠ J 9 7 6 ♥ 5 2 ♦ K 10 7 ♣ A Q 9 2

SOUTH: ♠ A K 10 5 2 ♥ A K J 8 3 ♦ Q 4 ♣ J

Suggested Bidding	**WEST**	**NORTH**	**EAST**	**SOUTH**
				1♠
	Pass	Pass	Pass	

South has 18 high-card points plus 1 point for each of the five-card suits. That's not quite enough to start with a strong two-bid, so South opens 1♠. West's hand isn't good enough for an overcall and North doesn't have enough to respond 1NT. So, the auction comes to East.

East has 10 high-card points and can expect that partner has some strength as well, since the opponents haven't bid beyond the one level. However, this isn't the time to make a balancing double. East doesn't have the right shape. East is short in hearts and has length in spades. East can reason that West might have taken some action over 1♠ if West were short in spades and had a good hand. Since West passed, it is unlikely that East-West are missing a game contract and it looks as though East-West's best spot is defending against 1♠. East should pass.

If East does take some balancing action, North-South may well reach a game contract in hearts. South will probably jump to 3♥ to show the maximum-strength hand and North, with a good hand for hearts, might raise to game.

Suggested Opening Lead

Against South's contract of 1♠, West has no clear-cut lead. West would probably lead the ♣4, fourth highest, hoping to find some help in the suit in partner's hand.

Suggested Play

In a spade contract South, has five losers. There are three spade losers, two diamond losers, and a club loser. Since declarer can afford six losers, the contract seems safe. Nevertheless, declarer has to keep control of the trump suit to make the hand.

Suppose the defenders start by leading two rounds of clubs. Declarer ruffs the second round of clubs and can draw two rounds of trump with the ♠A-K. Declarer should now leave the remaining two trumps outstanding and start taking the winners in the heart suit, letting the defenders take their two spade winners whenever they wish.

If South were to lead a third round of trumps, East would win and draw declarer's last trump. Now the defenders could take all their club winners and the ♦A-K to defeat the contract.

If South plays in a heart contract, declarer can make ten tricks, losing only two diamonds and a club since the spade losers can be ruffed in dummy.

Suggested Defense

The defenders do best to lead and continue leading clubs, hoping to run declarer out of trumps. This won't be very effective against a heart contract but could work well against a spade contract if declarer chooses to play three rounds of trumps, hoping the missing spades are divided 3-3. Because they are divided 4-2, East will be able to draw declarer's last trump and the defenders can take their remaining club winners and ♦A-K.

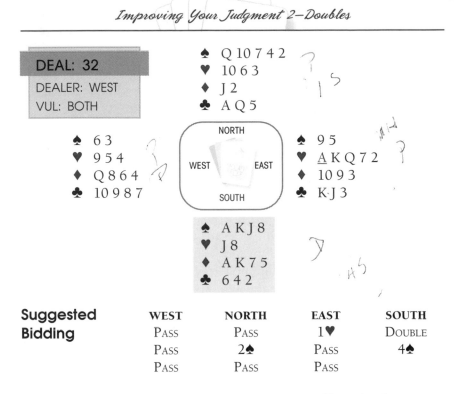

		♠ Q 10 7 4 2
		♥ 10 6 3
DEAL: 32		♦ J 2
DEALER: WEST		♣ A Q 5
VUL: BOTH		

NORTH

♠ 6 3		♠ 9 5
♥ 9 5 4	WEST EAST	♥ A K Q 7 2
♦ Q 8 6 4		♦ 10 9 3
♣ 10 9 8 7		♣ K J 3

SOUTH

♠ A K J 8
♥ J 8
♦ A K 7 5
♣ 6 4 2

Suggested	**WEST**	**NORTH**	**EAST**	**SOUTH**
Bidding	PASS	PASS	1♥	DOUBLE
	PASS	2♠	PASS	4♠
	PASS	PASS	PASS	

West and North pass. East opens the bidding 1♥ in third position. With 16 high-card points and support for the unbid suits, South makes a takeout double. West, despite the three-card heart support, doesn't have enough to raise to the two level with only 2 high-card points plus 1 dummy point for the doubleton spade.

North, with 9 high-card points plus 1 length point for the five-card suit, has enough to make an invitational jump to 2♠. South accepts the invitation and takes the partnership to the game level in spades.

Suggested Opening Lead

East is on lead against North's 4♠ and starts with the ♥A, top of the solid sequence.

Suggested Play

North has three heart losers and two club losers . . . two more than declarer can afford. One of the heart losers can be ruffed in dummy, so declarer's focus should be on avoiding two club losers.

One possibility is to try the club finesse, hoping West holds the ♣K. This is not likely to be successful since East opened the bidding and West didn't raise. A second possibility is to take a diamond finesse by leading toward the ♦J, hoping West holds the ♦Q. The order that declarer takes the finesses is important. If the diamond finesse doesn't work, declarer can still fall back on the club finesse. If the club finesse is taken first . . . and it doesn't work . . . it is too late to try the diamond finesse because a trick must be given up when leading toward the ♦J.

Suppose East takes two heart winners and then leads a trump. Declarer can win in dummy and lead a low diamond. If West plays low, declarer wins the ♦J and can later discard one club loser on the extra diamond winner in dummy. Declarer loses only two hearts and a club.

If West rises with the ♦Q and leads a club, declarer wins the ♣A. Declarer can then draw the remaining trumps and take a trick with the ♦J. Then declarer ruffs the remaining heart loser in dummy and plays the ♦A-K, discarding both club losers from the North hand. Declarer loses two heart tricks and a diamond.

What if East held the ♦Q? Declarer's diamond finesse would lose. Declarer could discard one club loser on the extra diamond winner in dummy and try the club finesse. If both finesses lose . . . bad luck.

Suggested Defense

East's best defense is to take two heart winners and then play a third high heart or a trump. East can't afford to lead a club, since that would give up a trick in that suit. Now declarer will have to take the diamond finesse rather than the club finesse to make the contract.

If East leads a diamond after taking the heart winners, declarer can make the hand by playing a low diamond from dummy. From declarer's perspective, this runs the slight risk that East has a singleton diamond and will get a ruff. To compensate, as long as East doesn't have a singleton diamond, playing low from dummy guarantees the contract. If East has the ♦Q, declarer will win a trick with the ♦J and can later discard a club loser on an extra diamond winner in dummy. If West wins the ♦Q, declarer will later take a trick with the ♦J and discard both club losers on dummy's remaining ♦A-K.

Glossary

Advancer—The partner of the player making a takeout double or an overcall. (page 27)

Balancing Position—The player in a position to make the final call when the opponents have stopped in a partscore contract. If the player in the balancing position passes, the auction is over. (page 86)

Balancing Takeout Double—A takeout double made in the balancing position. A balancing takeout double may be made with fewer values than in the direct position. (page 86)

Broken Sequence—A sequence of cards in a suit where the third card from the top is missing but not the next lower-ranking card(s). For example, ♥K-Q-10-9, ♦J-10-8. (page 18)

Competitive Auction—An auction in which both sides are bidding to try and win the contract. (page 1)

Convention—A bid which, by partnership agreement, conveys a meaning other than would normally be attributed to it. (page 2)

Cuebid—A forcing bid in a suit in which the bidder does not wish to play. Typically, it is a bid of the opponents' suit but it also refers to a control showing bid in a slam-going auction. (page 34)

Dangerous Opponent—An opponent that declarer does not want to gain the lead. The opponent may have winners to take or be in a position to make a damaging lead that could defeat the contract. (page 51)

Direct Position—A player in position to make a call immediately following an opponent's bid. (page 86)

Doubleton—A holding of two cards in a suit. (page 3)

Dummy Points—The valuation of shortness in a hand that is likely to be the dummy after a trump fit has been found: void - 5 points; singleton - 3 points; doubleton - 1 point. Dummy points are used in place of length points when making a takeout double. (page 3)

Duplicated Values—When too much of the combined partnership strength is concentrated in one place, usually leaving a weakness elsewhere. For example, if North holds the doubleton ♣A-Q and South holds the doubleton ♣K-J, the partnership has 10 high-card points in the suit but only two tricks. (page 37)

Forcing Bid—A bid that partner is not expected to pass. (page 28)

Higher-ranking Suit—Spades is the highest-ranking suit, followed by hearts, then diamonds, with clubs being the lowest-ranking suit. When advancing a takeout double with a choice of four-card suits, the higher-ranking suit is usually bid first, leaving advancer the flexibility to bid the lower-ranking suit later if the auction continues. This is contrary to responding to an opening bid when responder usually bids the lower-ranking suit first. (page 28)

Interior Sequence—A holding in a suit that contains a sequence and a higher-ranking card that is not part of the sequence. For example, ♥A-J-10-9, ♦Q-10-9-8. (page 51)

Invitational Bid—A bid which encourages partner to continue bidding but doesn't insist on another bid. (page 29)

Level—The number of tricks the partnership contracts to take when it makes a bid. It includes an assumed six tricks, so a bid at the three level represents a contract to take nine tricks. (page 3)

Loser on a Loser—Discarding a card that must be lost on a losing trick in another suit. This technique can be useful in many situations. (page 47)

Negative Double—The conventional use of responder's double of an opponent's overcall as a takeout double rather than a penalty double. This used to require partnership agreement but has become the standard treatment in tournament and club games. (page 95)

Passed Hand—A hand that passed when it had an opportunity to open the bidding and, therefore, is assumed to hold fewer than 13 points. The term may be applied to a hand which passes after the auction has started but, in that situation, the passed hand may hold 13 or more points but be unsuitable for making a bid at that point in the auction. (page 92)

Passout Position—A player in the position to end the auction by passing. (page 86)

Penalty Double—A double made with the intention of increasing the bonus for defeating the opponents' contract. Partner is expected to pass. (page 1)

Preemptive Jump Raise—A raise of partner's suit skipping one or more levels. By agreement, this can be used to show a weak hand with good trump support in a competitive auction. (page 18)

Preemptive Bid—A bid made to interfere with the opponents' auction. As an opening bid or an overcall, it is usually made with a long suit and a weak hand by skipping one or more levels in the auction. (See also Preemptive Jump Raise.) (page 22)

Redouble—A bid that increases the scoring value of tricks and penalties after an opposing double. After an opponent's takeout double of opener's bid, responder's redouble is typically used to show a hand of about 10 or more points, sending the message: "The hand belongs to our side." (page 36)

Reopening Double—A double made by a player in the passout position. (page 94)

Responder—The partner of the opening bidder. The partner of a player who has made an overcall or takeout double is preferably referred to as the advancer rather than the responder to avoid ambiguity. (page 27)

Responsive Double—The conventional use of a double by advancer for takeout when responder raises opener's suit following a takeout double. This is not the standard treatment of advancer's double and it requires partnership agreement. (page 40)

Sacrifice—Bidding to a contract which isn't expected to make to prevent the opponents from playing and making their contract. If the penalty for being defeated is less than the value of the contract the opponents could have made, the sacrifice is successful. (page 126)

Singleton—A holding of one card in a suit. (page 3)

Solid Sequence—Three or more consecutive cards in a suit, headed by an honor. For example, ♥K-Q-J-10, ♦Q-J-10-5. (page 23)

Takeout Double—A double which requests partner to bid rather than pass. (page 1)

Truscott 2NT—The conventional use of a jump to 2NT by responder to show the values for a limit (invitational) raise after opener's suit has been doubled for takeout. A corollary of this agreement is that responder's jump raise of opener's suit is preemptive following a takeout double. (See Preemptive Jump Raise.) (page 80)

Unbid Suit—A suit that has not been bid by either side during the auction. (page 2)

Void—A holding of zero cards in a suit. (page 3)

Vulnerability—The status of a hand during a round of bridge which affects the size of the bonuses scored for making or defeating contracts. Neither side may be vulnerable; one side may be vulnerable and the other side non vulnerable; or both sides may be vulnerable. (page 3)

Wasted Values—High cards or distributional values that do not contribute to the offensive trick-taking potential of the partnership hands. (See Duplicated Values.) (page 11)